THE

HISTORY

OF THE

ARISH OF GARSTANG

IN THE

COUNTY OF LANCASTER.

BY

LT.-COLONEL HENRY FISHWICK, F.S.A.,

Author of " The History of the Parochial Chapelry of Goosnargh,"
" The History of the Parish of Kirkham,"
" The Lancashire Library," &c.

PART I.

PRINTED FOR THE CHETHAM SOCIETY.
M.DCCC.LXXVIII.

PREFACE

IN presenting to the members of the Chetham Society what I may call another Chapter in the History of Amounderness, I have few introductory remarks to make. The parish of Garstang is — next to the parish of Kirkham — the largest in the hundred, and from its situation, antiquity and surroundings, it was thought that its records could not fail to yield much that would be interesting to the historian and genealogist. In this respect my hopes have been more than realized, as I venture to think the following pages will show. Every available source of information has been consulted, and no effort has been spared to exhaust the subject without printing what would be of little or no value. I am greatly indebted to many owners of land in Garstang and possessors of title-deeds and other manuscripts relating to the parish, whose names will be found in the foot notes of the History; but I am under special obligation to the following gentlemen, and I wish here to record my sense of it, viz: the Rev. WILSON PEDDER, M.A., vicar of Garstang; the Rev. W. ARMITSTEAD, of St. Thomas's, Garstang; the Rev. J. D. BANISTER, late incumbent of Pilling; the Rev. J. W. WAITHMAN, M.A., vicar of Pilling; Lord WINMARLEIGH; JAMES NICHOLSON,

Esq., F.S.A., of Warrington; RICHARD PEDDER, Esq., of
Ulverston; RICHARD VEEVERS, Esq., of Preston, and the
Bailiff and Burgesses of the town of Garstang.   To my
friends J. E. BAILEY, Esq., F.S.A., of Stretford; J. P.
EARWAKER, Esq., F.S.A., of Withington; Colonel J. L.
CHESTER, LL.D., of London, and WILLIAM BEAMONT,
Esq., of Orford hall, I also tender my sincere thanks for
kindly assistance.

H. F.

Carr Hill, Rochdale,
December 1878.

CONTENTS OF PART I.

ILLUSTRATIONS.

THE

HISTORY OF GARSTANG.

CHAPTER I.

ERRATA.

Page 9, note, *for* "Gallas" *read* "Gallus."

,, 23, line 22, *for* "Fily" *read* "Fitz."

,, 24, ,, 12, *for* "Ricihale" *read* "Ricihale's."

,, 34, note 110, *for* "viccœm" *read* "vicecom."

,, 43, line 21, *for* "Rowall" *read* "Wynmerlegh."

,, 44, ,, 9, *for* "Thornond" *read* "Thomond."

,, 57, ,, 23, *for* "Rignayden" *read* "Rigmayden."

,, 64, ,, 8, *for* "Wakerfield" *read* "Wakefield."

,, 95, ,, 21, *for* "cvnctus" *read* "cvntis."

dale; and contained an area of 28,881 statute acres.

Of the state of this district prior to the great *Domesday Survey* we have no record except such as may be afforded by the few ancient remains which have, from time to to time, been exhumed, and to some of which enthusiastic antiquaries have assigned a pre-Roman date. We think, however, that stronger evidence is required to warrant a positive assertion on the subject, and shall

B

HISTORY OF GARSTANG.

CHAPTER I.

GENERAL HISTORY.

WITH the exception of Kirkham, Garstang is the largest parish in the Hundred of Amounderness ; on its south lie the parishes of St. Michael's-le-Wyre and Broughton, and the township of Myerscough ; on the east is the parish of Goosnargh and the Forest of Bleasdale; its western boundary is formed by the townships of Hamilton (part of Kirkham parish), Preesall with Hackensall, Stalmine with Stainall, and the parish of Cockerham ; and its northern boundary is formed by the parish of Lancaster.

Garstang, as originally constituted, consisted of the following townships, viz.: Barnacre with Bonds, Bilsborrow, Cabus, Catterall, Claughton, Cleveley (part), Forton (part), Garstang, Holleth (part), Kirkland, Nateby, Pilling (part), Winmarleigh, and Nether Wyersdale; and contained an area of 28,881 statute acres.

Of the state of this district prior to the great *Domesday Survey* we have no record except such as may be afforded by the few ancient remains which have, from time to to time, been exhumed, and to some of which enthusiastic antiquaries have assigned a pre-Roman date. We think, however, that stronger evidence is required to warrant a positive assertion on the subject, and shall

B

content ourselves with a brief description of the various "finds" which have been made.

It will be well to bear in mind that nearly all authorities agree that a Roman road passed through Bilsborrow and Claughton, and that the site of it in the latter place is still known as "Fleet street."

In 1856, near the southern base of Bone or Bon hill in Pilling during an excavation there, the foundation of an ancient habitation was discovered. It consisted of a circular trench of about eighteen inches wide, nearly twenty inches deep, and four yards in diameter; upon the enclosed space the clay excavated had been thrown and had become converted into a dry disintegrated sand. The remains of trees and wood around had been charred by fire, and charcoal was scattered about; and near to the circle a considerable quantity of hazel and alder poles was found, and not far distant, as the farmer described it, a "hatful of nuts." Bonehill, although now two miles above high-water mark, stands on the verge of an ancient sea beach.[1]

In Pilling Moss about a mile and a half of an ancient causeway has been traced, which is known by the name of Dane's Pad, and about which there is a diversity of opinion, some maintaining that it is of Roman origin, and others that it is nothing more or less than the remains of a foot path made by the monks of Cockersand Abbey as a means of access to their large possessions in Rawcliffe and the neighbourhood.

The direction of the path is in a straight line from Pilling Hall to Hales Hall in Rawcliffe, and it is now several feet below the surface of the moss; it is formed of large oak trees riven or sawn asunder, and laid upon sleepers to which the trees are fastened by wooden pegs going through the sleepers into the ground; its width is from fourteen to twenty inches.[2]

---

[1] The Rev. J. D. Banister (*vide* Hewitson's *Our Country Churches*).

[2] See *Trans. of Lanc. and Chesh.*, Hist. Soc., pp. 111, 120. Another path, called "Kate's Pad," Mr. Thornber states tradition says, was formed by two ladies to obtain snuff with expedition from Lancaster.

At Cogie Hill in Winmarleigh, some years ago, was dug up an oak box fastened together with oak pins, which contained several celts, arrow heads, &c., which are now deposited in the Warrington Museum, and which are thus described by Mr. H. Syer Cuming :

"The largest is perhaps one of the finest examples that has been brought to light and is in excellent preservation. It measures upwards of nineteen inches in length.

"The Socket, which is one inch and three-sixteenths in diameter at the base, extends up the centre of the leaf-shaped blade to its apex. The edges are ground thin : and the blade is perforated on each side of the socket towards the lower part with an 'eye' two inches and three-sixteenths long. This specimen is in fact an example of what is called in the Irish story 'slidh cheann-ramhar chro-fhairsing catha,' the heavy-headed broad-eyed spear of battle : a form, however, which is found in north and south Britain, as well as in Hibernia.

"The second spear-head is of a much smaller size and less ornate character than its gigantic companion. It is nearly eight inches and a half long.

"The edges of its leaf-shaped blade are ground sharp, the socket extends to the very point, and measures one inch in diameter at the base : and like the socket of the first specimen is perforated for the admission of a peg or rivet which secured it to the staff of ashwood."

Here were also found five specimens of what are commonly called "socketed celts," which have each a loop at one side, their faces being decorated with a tridental figure.[3]

The writer of the above thinks that probably these brazen arms owe their origin to the confederate Voluntii and Sistunii ; powerful tribes of Brigantes, who had the county towards the close of British independence.

At Claughton, 1822, in constructing a new road near Claughton

---

[3] Pamphlet "on British Antiquities discovered in Lancashire" and deposited in the Warrington Museum. G. H. Syer Cuming, Esq.

Hall, some workmen in cutting through a small hill or tumulus of sand about three or four feet from the surface, came upon two large convex brooches joined together and forming a sort of oval box. They were of white metal, perforated in an ornamental pattern. The box contained two beads of coloured paste, one of blue and one of red, and a molar tooth.

The brooch itself had been enclosed in a wooden case which had apparently been lined with cloth. At the same place was found an iron axe and hammer, a stone axe, maul head, an iron spear head, and an iron sword, all of which were in a wooden case. Also an urn of baked clay containing charred bones.[4]

We are not inclined to assign a greater antiquity to these remains than the time when Northumbria was held by the Danes, or at the farthest, the period of the Saxon Heptarchy.

If the Romans had a settlement in the parish of Garstang, whether on the unfathomable moss of Pilling or in the primeval forests of Wyresdale, long ere this some indisputable trace would have been found.

The Saxons and the Danes have left traces behind them— if in nothing else — in the names of places.

The great *Domesday Survey* furnishes the following particulars about the parish :

"Aschebi [? Nateby] one carucate : Cathrehala [Catterall] two carcutes : Clactune [Claughton] two carucates : Bileuurde [Bilsborough] two carucates : Fortune [Forton] one carucate : Cherestang [Garstang] six carucates."

Assuming that Aschebi was intended for Nateby, and including the whole of Forton, this only gives about 1400 acres as under cultivation at this time, nearly half of which was in the township of Garstang, whilst the township in which the church stood (if it was then in existence) is not even mentioned, unless we suppose that "Cherestang" included Kirkland, and in that case it is not improbable that Baines is correct in translating the name as "church-pool."

---

[4] Paper read to Soc. of Ant. by Michael Jones, Esq., F.S.A. (*Arch. Journal*, vol. vi, p. 74.

Of the condition of Garstang during the twelfth century no record has been preserved; it had, however, as early as 12 Hen. III. [1226–27], given its name to a family, as a Paulinus de Gairestang was one of the knights who perambulated the Lancashire forests[5] (see chap. vii.)   At this time the manor was part of the possessions of the Lancastres, barons of Kendal and Wyersdale, and had, no doubt, been held by them for some years, as William de Lancastre, who was steward to Henry II.[6] made a grant of four bovates of land in the vill of Gairstang, with the dead wood of Kirklonde, to the abbots of Cockersand Abbey, to hold as of their church of St. Helen's (see chap. ii.); he also gave to the monks and their tenants, housebot and haybot in Kirklonde and Wyresdale, and other privileges[7] which were confirmed by Gilbert, the son of Roger fitz Reinfrid, his son-in-law.[8]

By deed without date, "William de Lancastre gave to Richard le Botiller the mill of Gayrstang with its site and pool to hold by homage and service." To this deed the witnesses were "Dnā Agnetè de Lancastr' spousa mea," and "Gregorie de Wymmerley," and others.[9]   :

In 31 Hen. III. (1246–47) William de Lancastre, the third baron, died without issue, seized of Scotforth, Kirkelond, Withall, Gayrestang and Warton; Agnes, his widow, held Garstang as her dower, which descended to Peter de Brus and Walter de Lindsey, his nephews and heirs.[10]   Peter de Brus was the son of Helewise de Lancastre, the eldest sister of William de Lancastre; and Walter de Lindsey was the son of Alice, his second sister; Sarrota, the third sister, married Alan de Multon, and died *s.p.*

On the division of the estate the manor of Garstang passed to the Lindseys, which family terminated in an heiress, Christiana

[5] *Lansd. MSS.*, 559, p. 55.

[6] *Jovenal Apud. Dugd. Baron.*, vol. i, p. 421.

[7] *Confirm.*, 7 and 8 Ric. II., N. 1; and *Coucher Book of Cockersand.* The *Coucher Book* is now lost; all efforts to trace it have failed.

[8] Baines' *Lanc.*, vol. ii, p. 257.

[9] Dodsworth's *MSS.*, vol. liii.

[10] *Inq. Post. Mort.*

de Lindsey, who married Ingelram de Ghisna, lord of Coucy in France,[11] who, in 20 Edward I. (1291–92) was called on by a writ of *quo warranto* to show why he and Christiana, his wife, held a market, assize of bread and ale, gallows and infangthef in Warton and Gayrestang, the right to hold which belonged to the crown.

Christiana's attorney pleaded that the market was held in Warton only, and that the rights exercised in Garstang were such as William de Lancastre had died seised of. The attorney for the crown attempted to prove that a market was also held in Garstang, but failed, and therefore the jury confirmed the rights of the defendants.[12]

John de Blackburn of Wiswall, had a daughter and coheiress who married Sir Robert Sherburne, whose daughter Katherine married, according to one authority,[13] a Tempest of Bracewell, but who was probably twice married, one husband being Sir John Haverington of Farleton, who died in 1362, seised of, in right of his wife Katherine, certain lands and tenements in Garstang and Winmerlegh, held as of the manor of Wyersdale, which lands, &c., descended to his son, Sir Thomas Haverington, who died so seised 38 Edward II. (1364–65).[14]

Ingelram de Ghisna, the eldest son of the Lord of Coucy, was created Earl of Bedford 40 Edward III. (1366–67), and dying in (22 Ric. II.) 1398–9 left his estates to Philippa, Duchess of Ireland, who died without issue, but previous to her death a warrant, dated 9 Nov., 1411, was directed to the auditors of the duchy accounts instructing them to certify to the council whether she was entitled to assize of ale in the township of Garstang.[15]

In 34 Edward III. (1360) Garstang, with its members, belonged

[11] *Notitia Cestriensis*, vol. ii, p. 408.

[12] *Plac. de Quo Warranto*, Lanc., Rot. 10.

[13] Pedigree of Sherburne quoted by Baines, who erroneously states that Robert de Blackburn held Garstang before the time of Edward I. He held Garston in West Derby, in right of his wife Ellen (see Three *Lanc. MSS.*, Cheth. Soc., vol. lxxiv, p. 31).

[14] *Inq. Post. Mort.*

[15] *Record Office Warrants*, 11 and 12 Hen. IV., fol. 9b.

to Henry, Duke of Lancaster,[16] whose descendant held it probably for some years, but at the same time there existed several
subfeudatory lords.   The Multons, who descended from Sarotta,
the sister of William de Lancastre, retained lands here, and (by
deed without date) Hu., son of H. de Multon de Garstang,
conveyed to Hu. de Multon two bovates of land in Garstang for his homage, and an annual rent of one pound of
cinnamon at the Feast of the Nativity of the Virgin.[17]

William Twenge, the son of Marmaduke de Twenge, who
married Lucy, the daughter and coheir of Peter Brus, died
15 Edw. III. (1341–42) seised of a fourth part of knight's fee in
Garstang, and his brother and heir, Thomas de Twenge, held
certain wastes, called Salome.[18]   The *Inq. Post Mort.* on his
death was taken in 48 Edw. III. (1374–75), when he was seised of
four messuages and 30 acres of land in the town of Garstang, and
his heirs were Isabella, wife of Walter Penwarden, and daughter of
Margareta (sister to the said Thomas Twenge); John de Hothorn
de Scorborgh, son of Madilda, another daughter of Margareta's ;
Elizabeth, wife of William Botereaux, and daughter of Katherine,
sister to Margareta and Robert de Lumley, son of Marmaduke de
Lumley, who married a daughter of Lucia, sister to Thomas de
Twenge.[19]

In 30 Edw. III. (1356–57) Sir William le Mollineux married
Joane, the daughter and heiress of Jordan Ellolt and Alice his
wife, daughter of Thomas Twenge, who was then forester of
Wyersdale.[20]   In 10 Hen. VI. (1431–32) Sir John de Lumley
died seised of 4 messuages 33 acres of land in Garstang, and a
messuage and 50 acres called Sulan.[21]

William de Coucy (second son of Ingelram de Gynes), and

---

[16] *Inq. Post. Mort.*

[17] Kuerden's *MSS.* (Heralds Coll.), vol. iv, fol. G, 1; and *Testa de Nevill*, fol. 397.

[18] *Inq. Post Mort.*, 15 and 18 Edw. III.

[19] *Inq. Post Mort.*, 48 Edw. III.

[20] Dodsworth's *MSS.*, 61 (1).   In another part of the same *MSS.* William le
Mollineux is called James, and Jordan Ellolt is called Jordan de Thwenge *alias* Ellale.

[21] A Wood in Barnacre is still known as "Sullum Wood."

Robert de Coucy de Gynes held, 20 Edw. III. (1346–47), in Garstang, a mill, as well as lands, &c., in Wyersdale, Kirkland, and other parts of the parish (see *post*). William de Coucy died without male heirs, and his estate here went to the crown, he had held a carve of land by the fourth part of a knight's fee, paying yearly 2*s.* 6*d.* at the Nativity of John the Baptist,[22] which in 1349 was granted, by Edw. III., to Sir John de Coupeland and Johanna his wife (who was the widow of William de Coucy, and according to one account, daughter and heiress of John Rigmayden[23]), with remainder to Ingelram de Coucy, who married the king's daughter. Johanna died in 49 Edw. III. seised of Kirkland.[24] John de Coupeland was a distinguished soldier; at the battle of Neville's Cross, near Durham (which took place on the 17 Oct., 1347), he took prisoner the Scotch king, David II., for which he was knighted by Edw. III., who also granted him a pension of 500*l.* a year.[25]

In 1440 (23 Aug.) a precept was issued to the escheator of the county to give livery and seisin to Nicholas Rigmaden, son and heir of Thomas Rigmaden, of an eighth part of the manor of Garstang which his father held in fee, and other lands and tenements which were held conjointly with Alice his wife, taking security for the payment of his relief.[26]

It is most probable that now, and for some time previous, the real owner of the greatest part of the manor was the abbot and convent of Cockersand, to whom the minor lords owed fealty and service, and that it continue as part of the possessions of the monastry until the dissolution.

The following extracts from the Bursar Roll of the Cockersand Abbey will show the property which the abbot and convent held in this parish.

---

[22] *Lancashire Survey* (Cheth. Soc., vol. lxxiv, p. 53).
[23] *Lansd. MSS.*, 559, fol. 35.
[24] *Inq. Post Mort.*
[25] *Froissail Chronicle.*
[26] *Thirtieth Report of Deputy Keeper of Public Records*, p. 213.

BURSAR'S RENT ROLL, 1451.[27]

Gayrstang Sm̄ᵃ.[28]

Ricūs Cartmale tȝ ɪ ten⁹ in gayrstang r⁹ ꝑ An^m vi gˢ [29]	xviˢ
Vicar⁹ de gayrstang tȝ ɪ ten⁹ ibim vi gˢ.........	xviiiˢ
Margar⁹ Pylkyngton tȝ ɪ toft rȝ ij gˢ............	xxᵈ
Jōh Clerkson tȝ ɪ ten⁹ rȝ iiij gˢ	viijˢ viijᵈ
Jōh Strekett tȝ ɪ ten⁹ & ɪ cot ix gˢ	xxiiijˢ viijᵈ
Id : Jōh tȝ ɪ cot r⁹	ijˢ
Roƀrt Browne tȝ ɪ ten⁹ & ɪ cot⁹ r⁹ vii gˢ	xxˢ viᵈ
Id roƀrt tȝ ɪ ten⁹ qn'od in tent⁹ her⁹ Grwome r⁹ iiij gˢ	viˢ
Thom̄s Walton tȝ ɪ ten⁹ r⁹ iij gˢ..................	xijˢ viijᵈ
Ric̄ Smyth tȝ ɪ ten⁹ r⁹ iij gˢ	vijˢ
Thom̄s Smyth tȝ ɪ ten⁹ r⁹ v gˢ	ixˢ
Thoms ffynch tȝ ɪ ten⁹ ɪ cot⁹ r⁹ vi gˢ	xiiijˢ
Roƀr̄t Clerk tȝ ɪ ten⁹ r⁹ iiij gˢ	viijˢ viijᵈ
Symond Rawthmell tȝ ɪ ten⁹ r⁹ vi gˢ	xiiijˢ
Jenet p̂mate tȝ ɪ cot⁹ r⁹ iij gˢ	iiijˢ
U᷑x Ric̄i pyp tȝ ɪ ten⁹ r⁹ iij gˢ.....................	viijˢ
Adam deconson tȝ ɪ cot⁹ r⁹ iij gˢ	iiijˢ
Jeneta rydar tȝ ɪ ten⁹ r⁹ iij gˢ	vˢ
Ric̄hˢ Dorhm̄ tȝ ɪ ten⁹ r⁹ vi gˢ	xiijˢ iiijᵈ
Henrˢ Gervesson tȝ ɪ ten r⁹ xii gˢ	xvˢ
Richˢ rygmagdyn tȝ Gylysholme & tylysholme r⁹ ꝑ An⁹.....................................	viˢ viijᵈ
lyngard her Jōh lyngard tȝ lyngard cū pt̄n lib⁹ ꝑ An⁹	viˢ viiiᵈ & xviij
Styhyrst Jōh Rogekynson tȝ tr⁹ nr̄am ad voln̄r	viᵈ
ferdesthaghll Jōh Edyfford tȝ t⁹ ad volu̅ voc̄ ferdesthagh	iijˢ iiijᵈ

[27] *MS.* belonging to Hornby Chapel House, furnished through the Rev. T. E. Gibson, the author of *Lydiate Hall and its Associations.*

[28] Smalemanland=land originally allotted to small tenants.

[29] Gallas, a cock. The monastery must have been well supplied with poultry.

Rowall   Rich⁵ Botler t₃ tr⁹ ad volū in Rowall .... iij⁵ iiij⁴
          Rog⁹ Adamson t₃ a⁹ ad volū pert⁹ ibm̄ r⁹...... vi⁴
          Ric⁹ Cat⁹all t₃ ı ten⁹ ibm̄ lib' r⁹................. xij⁴
Kyrkeland Ric⁹ Bottler t₃ tr⁹ in Kyrkeland vo⁹ noncroft
          lib' r⁹ .... xij⁴
Sterysacre her Laur Sterysacr t₃ lib' ibm̄ r⁹.................. xij⁴
Wym̄ly   Jōh rowell³⁰ t₃ ı ten⁹ in Wynm⁹ly ad volū r⁹
          vi g⁵ .... ix⁵
          Robrt ffox t₃ ı ten⁹ ibm lib' r⁹ p an⁹ .... ij⁵ vi⁴
                        Forton Smᵃ.
          Evan Walsman t₃ ı ten⁹ in fforton r p an vi g⁵ x⁵   ij mess
          Jōh Chatburne t₃ ı ten⁹ & ı cot⁹ r⁹ viii g⁵ ... xvii⁵   iij mess
          Ux Jōh don⁹dale t₃ ten⁹ r⁹ ij g⁵ .... iiij⁵ viil⁴ ij mess
          Robr̄t ffycher remor t₃ ı ten⁹ cū ı claus⁹ voc
          laykemor⁹ vi g⁵.............................. xix⁵ viij⁴
          Do. robrt t₃ ı cot⁹ r⁹ .... xvi⁴
          Do. robrt t₃ ı claus⁹ vo⁹ kar meadow r⁹ ... v⁵
          Jōh Bond t₃ ı ten⁹ r⁹ vi g⁵ .... xv⁵ ij mess
          Jōh Brone t₃ ten⁹ cu⁹ claus⁹ vo baghyrst r⁹
          viij g⁵ .... xx⁵   ij mess
          Jōh Cutfox t₃ ı ten⁹ r⁹ vi g⁵ .... xv⁵   ij mess
          Jōh Clerkson t₃ ı ten⁹ r⁹ vi g⁵ .... xiiij⁵   ij mess
          Jōh hogeson t₃ ı ten⁹ r vi g⁵ ....· xx⁵   ij mess
          Robrt Mawdysley t₃ ı ten⁹ r vi g⁵.............. xiij⁵ iiij⁴ ij mess
          Id robt t₃ ı claus⁹ vo⁹ grenefall .... iiij⁵
          Id: robrt t₃ ı claus⁹ qu'd: in ten⁹ Willi carne iij⁵
          Joh redar t₃ ı ten⁹ r⁹ iiij g⁵³¹ .... xi⁵ ii mess
          Wills Belane t₃ ı ten r⁹ vi g⁵ .... xvi⁵   ii mess
          Henr⁵ Curwen t₃ ı ten⁹ r⁹ vi g⁵ .... xii⁵   ii mess
          Ux: Jōh Dawson t₃ ı ten⁹ r⁹ v g⁵............... v⁵   i mess

³⁰ 27 Hen. 8. Edwad Roo *alias* Rowale died seized of land and wood in Winmarleigh (*Inq. Post. Mort.*) A place is still known as "Rooa."
³¹ In 6 Edw. VI (1552-53). Richard Reeder was plaintiff, and Rich. Harryson
and Elizabeth Harryson, widow, were defendants in a cause touching the title to certain
lands in the manor of Forton held of the late Abbey of Cockersand (*Cal. to Plead.*)

John paton t₃ ı ten r vi gˢ .... xvˢ   ij mess
Lauʳ⁹ Chernoke t₃ ı acrᵖ trᵖ ibm rᵖ .... xviᵈ
Willˢ Carne t₃ ı tenᵖ rᵖ viij gˢ .... viˢ   ii mess
Robtᵖ ffyscher Junior t₃ ı tenᵖ rᵖ iiij gˢ ...... xiiˢ viiiᵈ iij mess
Willˢ ffysher t₃ ı tenᵖ rᵖ viij gˢ .... xiijˢ iiijᵈ iij mess
Henrˢ Corlehous t₃ ı *Acrciamsᵗ* rᵖ .... viᵈ

Libᵖ Tenenᵖ in fforton.

Rogᵖ Brekdannes t₃ ı tenᵖ in fforton libe rᵖ... ijᵈ
Jōh Caton t₃ ı tenᵖ ibm̄ libe rᵖ .... xilijᵈ
Will Ambrose t₃ ı clausū ibm̄ libe voᵖ poot-
        field rᵖ .... ijᵈ
Henrᵖ Corlehous t₃ ı tenᵖ ibm̄ libe rᵖ .... xiiᵈ
   Do. Henrᵖ t₃ altᵖ ibm̄ libe rᵖ .... xᵈ
Jōh Dobmagh t₃ ı tenᵖ libe rᵖ .... xvᵈ
Ux : Henricᵖ Hogeson t₃ ı tcnᵖ ibm̄ rᵖ......... xviijᵈ
Lauʳ⁹ Chernoke t₃ ı tenᵖ ibm libe rᵖ............ ijˢ iiijᵈ
her Jōh richardson t₃ ı tenᵖ ibm libe rᵖ......... iiˢ viᵈ
Will Belan t₃ trᵖ ibm libe rᵖ .... iiijᵈ
Rogᵖ ffysher t₃ ı tenᵖ ibm libe rᵖ .... vᵈ
herᵖ Johᵖ Wyrysdale t₃ trᵖ ibm libe rᵖ .... iiijᵈ
Joh Calfson t₃ trᵖ ibm libe rᵖ .... iᵈ
Joh Spimke t₃ ı tenᵖ ibm libe rᵖ .... xᵈ
Joh perrsage t₃ trᵖ ibm libe rᵖ .... xviᵈ   .
Henᵖ Sharpall rᵖ ꝑ anᵐ .... ijᵈ

Bursar' Rent Roll; 1501.³²

Nicoll Gervas t₃ t' r̄ vi gall'........................ xviˢ
Ricᵖ Stowt t₃ t' r̄ vi gallᵖ........................... xxˢ
Robt Port' t₃ t r̄ ix gallᵖ .... xxiiiiˢ viiiᵈ
Vx Willᵃᵐ Gervase t₃ t' r̄ .... xxᵈ
Thomas Chatburne t₃ t' r̄ vi gallᵖ .... xxᵈ
Vx Nicolai Sylkok t₃ t' r̄ vij gall .... xxˢ
Idm vx t₃ ẗ' vocat Clerke Fyld r̄ iiij gallᵖ ... viˢ
Vx Robti Milton t₃ ẗ r̄ vj gallᵖ .... xijˢ viiiᵈ

John Dorem t₃ t̄ r̄ vi gall⁹ .... ixˢ

Rog⁹ Smith t₃ t̄ r̄ vi gall............................ xiiijˢ

Rog⁹ Tomlynson t₃ t̄ r̄ iii gall⁹ .... viiˢ

Vx Thoms Strekett t₃ t̄ r̄ vj gall⁹ .... viiiˢ viiiᵈ

Rog⁹ Rawthmell t₃ t̄ r̄ iiii gall⁹ .... xviˢ

Thomas Bradley t₃ t̄ r̄ iii gall⁹ .... iiiiˢ

Robt Dorem t₃ t̄ r iiii gall⁹ .... viiˢ

Vx Robt Wylkynson t₃ t̄ r iii gall⁹ .... vˢ

Henr̄ Dorem t₃ t̄ r̄ vi gall⁹ .... xiiiˢ iiiiᵈ

Vx Johis Gerves t₃ t̄ r iiii gall⁹ .... xiˢ iiiiᵈ

Jamys Gerves t₃ t̄ r viii gall⁹ .... xxviiiˢ viiiᵈ

Will'm Hedsforth & fili⁹ ciu⁹ Wittᵍ tent t'
     vocat' Perthyng Hall alit' dict Abbot
     Skale .... iiiˢ iiiiᵈ

Jamys Clerkson t₃ in wymnlegh r̄ vi gall⁹ ...... ixˢ

John Rygnayden t₃ Gyllysholme t̄ Tyllysholme viiiˢ viiiᵈ

Jacob₃ Butler t₃ in Rohall r .... iiiˢ iiiiᵈ

Will'm Adamson t₃ t̄ iuxᵃ Tendberne³³ ad
     volut'r.. viᵈ

Radulfus Cat'all t₃ in Cat'all lib. r̄............... xiiᵈ

Wil'n Butler t₃ i kyrkland vocat' Uncrofte &
     Bolandwra r̄ .... xiiᵈ

Her̄ Laurenē Steyrsacr̄ t₃ t̄ voc' Brademede
     lib. mᵒ i tenur̄ Thome, Ric. & hered Johis
     Walkar de lancastˢ r̄........................ xiiᵈ

Edmnᵈ Caton t₃ t̄ in Wyresdale vocal' *Sty-
hyrste* r̄ .... viᵈ

John ffox t₃ ii t' in Wynmerlegh lib r̄......... iiˢ viᵈ

..... fili' Rog'i Brokhallst₃ Carlands i byrewith³⁴
     lib .... iiiˢ viᵈ

Henr̄ ffaryngton t₃ lyngard lib r̄ .... viˢ viiiᵈ

---

[33] Tythbarn.   [34] Byrworth (see *Post*).

FFORTON.[35]

Vx Ric'. Gardn' t̃ Iohēs filius eiu' tent t' vocat Horegard place r̃ viii gall⁹	xiii^s	iiii	mess
Johñ ffyscher t₃ r̃ viii gall⁹	xiii^s iiii^d	iii	mess
Will'm m'geryson t₃ t̃ viii gall'	xii^s iiii^d	iii	mess
Xp̄ofur Styholme t₃ t r̃ ii gall'	v^s	i	mess
Ric. Brade t₃ t' r̃ vi gall'	xii^s	ii	mess
Vx Johis Bonde t₃ t r̃ vi gall'.....................	ix^s vi^d	ii	mess
Thomas Bonde t₃ t' r̃ vi gall⁹.....................	xv^s vi^d	ii	mess
Will'm Bonde t₃ t' r̃ vi gall⁹	xv^s	ii	mess
Ric. Bonde t₃ t' vocat' Baghyrste ā vi gall⁹ ...	xv^s x^d	ii	mess
Iđm Ric. t₃ i clau͠s vocat' Dawson fall r̃ vi gall'	v^s	i	mess
Jacob' Curwen t₃ t' r̃ ii gall'	x^s viii^d	iii	mess
Johñ Gyll t₃ t' r̃ vi gall'	xv^s viii^d	iii	mess
Ric. Gardn^r t₃ t r̃ vi gall'.....................	xix^s	ii	mess
Ric. Henresson t₃ t r̃ x gall'	xxvi^s x^d	iiii	mess
Roƀ ffyscher senior t₃ t' v gall'	xx^s	ij	mess
Will'n Kechen t₃ t r̃ vi gall'	xxij^s vi^d	iii	mess
Edm̄ud Rayner t₃ t' r̃ iiii gall'....................	xi^s	ii	mess
Jamys Dawson t₃ t' r̃	xviij^s iv^d		
John Cutfox t₃ t' r̃ iiii gall'......................	x^s	ii	mess
Jamys Charnok t₃ t' r̃ iiii grll⁹	x^s vi^d	ii	mess
John Smyth t₃ p' tur' ad volut' r̃	xvi^d		
Will'm Henreson t₃ p'to ad volūt' r̃	xvi^s		
Vx Roƀti Corlose t₃ trām nrām r̃	vi^d		

FREE TENANTS.

Johñ Brekawnse t₃ t' lib r̃ p añu	xiii^d
Iđm Johēs t₃ ad volut' j acr̃ terre arablm r̃ ...	xii^d
Her̃ Johis Caton t₃ t' lib' r̃	xiiii^d
Thome Corlose t₃ t' lib r̃............................	xii^d
Henr̃ Ċorlose t₃ t' lib r̃	ii^d
Thomas Bakhouse t₃ t' lib r̃	xiiii^d

[35] It is not possible now to select the Garstang tenants in Forton—all are here given.

Johñ Marsehall t₃ t' lib r̃............................ ii^s vi^d

Johñ ffyscher t₃ t' vocat Horchard place lib r̃. v^d

Johñ Charnoke t₃ t' lib r̃........................... ii^s iiii^d

Her̃ Johĩs Wyresdale t₃ t' lib r̃ .... iii^d

Radulfus Corney t₃ t' lib r̃ .... xii^d

Nicol Jacson t₃ t' lib mo^o in tenur̃ Johis
    Rygmadyn r̃ .... ii^d

Sm̃^a xii^li xi^s vi^d

By Indenture bearing date, 4th Dec., 30 Hen. VIII (1538).[36]
Robert the abbot and convent of Cockersand, let the manor of
Garstang with its appurtenances, together with a messuage
situate in Newbiggin in Lonsdale in the tenure of Christopher
Conder (with its appurtenances), for a term of 99 years, to John
Rigmaden, at the annual rental of x^li viii^s, the following being
free tenants :

Annual Rent.

The heirs of William Adamson a tenement near
          the Tithe Barn .... vi^d

„   „   John Butler de Kirkland "armiger"
          land in nunncrofte .... xii^d

„   „   Christopher Caton land in Wiresdale... vi^d

„   „   John Brockholes .... xviii^d

„   „   Henry Hodgekinson land in Wym'ley. ii^s vi^d

„   „   Nicholas ffarington for land called
          Lingard .... vi^s viii^d

„   „   Nicholas Butler de Rawcliffe "armiger" iii^s iiii^d

„   „   Richard Catterall........................... xii^d

„   „   Laurence Stirseck for a meadow called
          Brodemedowe .... xii^d

„   „   Thomas Rigmayden land called Brilles-
          holme and Tillesholme .... viii^s vi^d

---

[36] Exchequer Minister's Accounts.   30 and 31 Hen. VIII, No. 167, also *Harl.*
MSS., 608, fol. 4.

At the time of the dissolution of the monastry the manor went to the crown, and it was shortly afterwards made over to the Savoy Hospital in fee, with a saving right to all the tenants.[37]

In 4 and 5 Phillip and Mary (1557–8) Ralph Jackson, the master of the Savoy and perpetual chaplain of the hospital, leased the manor of Garstang to Henry Saville, Esq., for 99 years, from and after the expiration of the former lease (to John Rigmaden).[38]

Henry Saville[39] of Barroughby and Lupset, was high sheriff of Yorkshire in 1568, and from 1556 to 1567 was one of the "Council of the North." He married Jane, daughter and coheiress of William Vernon of Barroughby, and widow of Sir Richard Bozom, Knt., he died. in 1567 and was buried at Barroughby, and by his will dated 1st Jan. 1568 (and proved 16th May following), he left the lease of Garstang manor to his servant William Saville, who, on 2nd April 1574, assigned his interest in the lease to William Holden of Garstang, and gave a bond of 200 marks for performances of certain covenants named in the will. On 16 Oct. 1574, John Rigmayden of Wedacre, Esq., purchased the lease of the manor, and dying in 1587 it descended to his son and heir, Walter Rigmayden, whose administrators, 10 Feb. 1602, sold it to Sir Thomas Gerard of Gerard, Bromley, in the county of Stafford, Knight, who made an agreement with the tenants for the abolition of certain ancient customs of paying fines at the death of the lord or tenant. Sir Thomas Gerard (afterward Lord Gerard) died 6th October 1617, and by a codicil in his will devised all his property not mentioned in the body of the will (Garstang not being so mentioned) to the payment of his debts, &c., and the residue to his younger sons John and William, appointing as his

[37] The Savoy Hospital in London was founded by King Henry VII, and called the Hospital of St. John the Baptist, it consisted of a master and four brethren who were priests in holy orders, it was dissolved in 1553 and refounded by Queen Mary. The Savoy for a long time previously had been part of the Duchy possessions.

[38] Abstract of title to manor in possession of Mr. Joseph Gillow.

[39] *Saville Correspondence* (Camden Society, 1858). The Henry Saville whose Letters are here published was the great grandson of Sir George Saville, the son and heir of the above named Henry Saville.

executors Alexander Standish and Richard Green of Garstang, the former of whom dying shortly afterwards, the executorship of the will was left to Richard Green, who, in 1624 (17 Jan.), received from John and William Gerard a full release and discharge.[40]

The manor afterwards passed to Digby, fifth Baron Gerard, whose only daughter and heiress, Elizabeth, married James, Earl of Arran, the fourth Duke of Hamilton and first Duke of Brandon, who was killed in a duel with Lord Mohun, which took place in Hyde Park, London, on the 15 Nov. 1712.[41] This meeting must have been of a most determined character, as both the combatants were killed ; the Duke of Hamilton was wounded in three places, one of which was a sword cut on the left breast "2 inches broad and about eight inches deep," whilst Lord Mohun had a wound on the right side "penetrating obliquely the whole body and coming out on the left above his hip," and the "great artery in the right groin was cut." A coroner's inquest was held on the bodies, and a verdict of wilful murder was recorded against the principals and their seconds.[42]

In 1738 the lease of the manor expired, and thus it would again fall to the crown ; and George II., by Letters Patent, under the seal of his court of exchequer, dated 3 Feb. 1742, demised, granted, and to farm let, to William Hall of the Middle Temple, Esq., all "that the manor of Garstang, with the rights, members and appurtenances, together with all Lands, Tenements, Meadows, Pastures, Feedings, Rents, Reversions, Services and Hereditaments to the said manor belonging; and also all that messuage, &c., in Newbiggine in Lonsdale" (see p. 1) to hold for a term of

---

[40] Abstract of title.

[41] Baines and others give 16 Nov. 1713. This is not correct, as is proved by reference to *The Case at large of Duke Hamilton and the Lord Mohun*, &c., London, 1712, for which these particulars are extracted.

[42] General Macartney, one of the seconds, in 1716 surrendered himself to take his trial at the court of King's Bench, and was acquitted of "murder," but found guilty of manslaughter.

thirty-one years from "the Feast of St. Michael the Archangel, which was in the year 1737."

By indenture dated 16 August 1742, the Hon. Edward Walpole, Esq., became entitled to manor, &c., for the remainder of the term, and upon his surrendering the Letters Patent and the said premises to the king, the same were re-conveyed to him for a term of thirty-one years from the 21 Oct. 1751, at a yearly rent of 10*l.* 8*s.*

A representation was, however, made to the king that Garstang being a "market town and situate on the common high road from London to the west of Scotland, the improvement of the said town would be of public utility and greatly tend to the encouragement and increase of trade and manufactures in and about the said town, and also to the ease and benefit of the inhabitants of the eastward part of that populous county, who cannot so conveniently repair to any other market; but the said Edward Walpole being only possessed of the premises for the remainder of the term is discouraged from attempting to make such improvements." Accordingly an Act of Parliament was passed which enabled the king to[43] convey the manor, &c., in fee, to the said Edward Walpole, through whose daughter it descended to the present owner, the Rev. W. A. Walpole-Keppel, B.A., rector of Haynford in Norfolk.

A Court Baron[44] was formerly held on behalf of the lord of the manor twice a year, but it is now only held once a year, when the following officers are elected : a constable, assessors, house lookers, affeerers,[45] engine masters, fence lookers and pindar (see Nether Wyersdale, *post*).

---

[43] Act of Parliament "To enable His Majesty to grant the Inheritance of Garstang, &c."

[44] Not a Court Leet with view of Franck Pledge. A Court Baron is necessarily appended to every manor.

[45] Affeerers (from the French affier to affirm) are officers appointed to moderate the amercements in Courts Baron. It is their duty to declare on the amount they think the offender should pay.

The following is a copy of the Charge to the Jury :

Gentlemen of the Jury the Intent of a Court Baron. Is in the first place to set ease and quietness betwixt Lord and Lord if any difference arises touching their boundaries.

In the second place for setting ease and quietness between Lord and Tenants. And lastly between Tenant and Tenant, Neighbour and Neighbour, and that one of them should not wrong another, but that the person wronged if the value be under 40/– should here have a speedy remedy. And such small Trespasses and Offences are here punishable by Americaments and Relief given in a speedy way.

And first You are to Enquire if all the Suitors to this Court do appear to do their Services to the Lords Court, or if any one that owes Suit and Service to the Lords Court, and withdraws the Same, or neglects to Repair the Lords Housing they are here presentable for by his Steward and by You he is to have his Rights preserved.

If any of the Lords Tenants cut down without his License any Timber or other Trees, it is waste and presentable.

If any Suitor makes Pits in the highways or private neighbourhood ways or has drained or stopped any waters or ditches, or diverted them into a wrong course.

Or have Encroached upon the Lords wastes without Licence.

Or suffer Hogs to go out unyoked or unringed to the annoyance of their neighbours or if any ditches want scouring or Hedges cutting or falling betwixt neighbour and neighbour whereby any person's land is overflowed with water or otherwise damaged.

These and such like offences are here presentable, and you are diligently to enquire of these offences and such like as you yourselves know to be here presentable.

THE TOWNSHIPS OF GARSTANG.

BARNACRE-WITH-BONDS

cannot boast any great antiquity, but was doubtless formerly held as part of the manor of Nether Wyresdale. Baines[46]

---

[46] The authority quoted in the first edition is *Duchy Records,* vol. iii, No. 29, which in the second edition is altered to *Duc. Lanc.* vol. iii, No. 29—both are wrong.

erroneously states that this township was part of the possession
of Sir James Laurence, but neither in the *Inq. Post Mort.* held
on the death of Robert Laurence, 28 Hen. VI (1449-50), or Sir
James Laurence in 1501, is it once named.

According to an *Inquis.* taken at Lancaster, 11th Sep. 1516,
upon the death of Margaret, the wife of Nicholas Rigmayden, it
appears that certain lands and tenements in "*Berneacre*" were
parcel of the manor of "Wodeacre," and were the inheritance of
Thomas Rigmayden (grandson of the said Margaret), and held
of the Queen as of her Duchy of Lancaster,[47] and in the reign
of Phillip and Mary (1554-1558) John Rigmayden lodged a
Bill of Complaint in the Duchy Court, to the effect that certain
lands in Barnacre, forming part of the manor of Wodacre, ought
of right to have descended to him from his father Thomas
Rigmayden deceased, but that one John Rigmayden of Newhall
in Barnacre had entered upon the premises, and held possession
of the deeds, &c. The defendant denies having the deeds and
pleads that the complainant had conveyed the property to John
Rigmayden, his (defendant's) father, for a term of years yet to
come.[48]

In 35 Eliz. (1592-3) Sir Gilbert Gerard, Attorney General,
died, seised of lands and tenements in Barnacre,[49] which descended to the Duke of Hamilton, who sold Bonds in 1834 and
Barnacre in 1853 to Mr. Bashell.

In this township are the very ancient manors of Byreworth
and Wedicar or Woodacre, which will be noticed hereafter, as
well as "Dimples," the ancient seat of the Plesingtons (see
chapter vii).

In Barnacre are the ruins of Greenhalgh castle, which was
erected in 1490, under a license granted by the king to Thomas,
Earl of Derby, by which he and his heirs were empowered to
erect in Greenhalgh a building or buildings, with stone or other

---

[47] *Inq. Post Mort.* vol iv, No. 72.

[48] *Duchy Records,* vol. vii, No. 21.

[49] *Inq. Post Mort.*

materials, and to embattle, turrellate, crenelate, machicollate, or
otherwise fortify the same ; authority being at the same time
given to enclose a park, and to have in it free warren and chase.
Any person hunting in the park without the Earl's consent was
made liable to a penalty of 20*l.*[50]

Camden states that "Greenhaugh castle" was built by the Earl
of Derby "whilst he was under apprehension of danger from
certain of the nobility of this county who had been outlawed, and
whose estates had been given by Henry the Seventh ; for they
made several attempts upon him, and many inroads into his
grounds, till at last these feuds were extinguished by the temper
and prudence of that excellent person."[51]

During the civil wars the castle was garrisoned by James,
Earl of Derby, on behalf of the king, and was placed under the
governorship of Christopher Anderton, the son of Sir Christopher
Anderton of Lostock.[52]   In August 1644, Sir John Meldrum,
being at Preston with his parliamentary army, gave orders to
Colonel Dodding to march his regiment "home and to provide
himselfe to beleaguer Grenall castle then possessed by the
cavaliers" ; this siege was not brought to a successful issue until
the year following, as in May 1645 Lathom house and "Greenhaugh castle" are mentioned as amongst the strongholds, north
of the Trent, still holding out.[53]

The following account of the siege is from *A Discourse of the
War in Lancashire.*[54]

"Colonell Dodding with his Regiment with Major Joseph
Rigbies companies laid close siege to Grenall Castle keeping
their maine Guard at Garstang towne, Into which were gotten
many desperat Papists. Their Governour was one Mr. Anderton.
They vexed the country thereabouts extreamly, fetching in the
night time many honest men from their houses, making a com-

[50] License, Dodsworth *MSS.* vol. lxxxvii, fol. 346; also Kuerden *MS.* 4to, fol. 59.
[51] Camden (Gibson's) p. 975.
[52] The Rev. T. C. Gibson's *Lydiate Hall,* p. 61.
[53] Rushworth, pt. iv, vol. i, p. 22.   [54] Chet. Soc. vol. lxii, p. 60.

moditie of it. They sallied out oft upon the Leaguers and killed some. They stood it out stoutly all that winter (1644–5). The Country was put to extraordinary charges in maintayning the Northern men, who made a prey without pittie such abound-ance of Provision they weekly destroyed. The Leaguers had thought to have undermined the Castle and have blown it up with gunpowder, and great cost was spent about it to pioners but to no effect. The ground was so sandy it would not stand. At last this Anderton died,[55] and them there within being thereby discoradged, they were glad to come to a composition to deliver it vp upon conditions—which were that they might go to their own houses and be safe. It was ordered that the Castle should be demolished and made untenable, and all the timber taken out of it and sold, which was done. And soe it lyes ruinated. It was very stronge, and builded so that it was thot Impregnable with any ordenance whatsoever, having but one dore to it, and the Walls of an exceeding thickness and very well secured together."

In 1772, Pennent, in making his northern tour, notes a single tower, "the poor remains of Greenhaugh Castle," of which in 1780 a drawing was made by Roger Dewhurst of Halliwell, Esq., and which was engraved in Baines' *History of Lancashire*. Of this single tower very little is now left; as the castle originally stood it was of rectangular form, with a tower at each angle, the interval between the walls was fourteen yards on one side and sixteen on the other, the whole being surrounded by a moat.[56] It is now part of the estate of Lord Bective.

BILSBORROW.[57]

There is little reason to doubt that this is the "Bileuuarde" of the *Domesday Survey*, which had then two carucates of land

---

[55] Lord Castlemaine's *List of Roman Catholics, Noblemen, and Gentlemen*, mentions Captain Anderton and Captain J. Hothersall as having died at Greenhalgh Castle.

[56] Baines' *Lanc.* vol. iv, p. 534.

[57] The modern spelling is Bilsborrow, though it is often spelt Bilsborough.

under cultivation, or at all events not lying absolutely "waste."
Alan de Singleton, who was living in the reign of King John,
died seised of two bovates of land in "Billisburghere"; his *Inq.
Post. Mort.* was held 29 Hen. III (1244-5), which descended to
Joan his daughter (and heiress to her brother Thomas de
Singleton), who married Thomas Banastre,[58] whose son William
died 17 Edw. II (1323-4) seised of half the "vill of Billeworth,"
and in "Billisburgh" a messuage, twenty acres of land, and a
mill. Adam Banastre, his son and heir, is described as holding
the manor of Billisburgh by service and a rent of 2s.

Adam Banastre, Knight, died about the year 1348, and his
son and heir, Thomas Banastre, who was knighted in 1360, held
"Billesbourghe," which is reckoned as "half a carve of land," by
service of the 20th part of a knight's fee, paying yearly 2s. at
the four terms.[59]

In 14 Edw. III (1340-41) the assessor appointed to value for
the *Nonarum Inquisitiones* rated "Billesburgh" at xxˢ.

In 20 Edw. I (1291-92) the Prior of the Order of St. John of
Jerusalem was cited to shew by what right he claimed the
judging of thieves, assize of bread and ale, &c., in (amongst other
places in Amounderness) "Billsburgh." The abbot of Cockersand was also called upon to answer the same question.[60]

In 25 Edw. I (1296-97) Edmund, brother of Hen. I and Earl
of Lancaster, amongst his immense possessions in the county,
held in this township lands of the annual value of 2s.[61]

In 15 Edw. I (1286-87) Roger de Byllesburgh appeared at
Lancaster at a forest assize as one of the "viridar," or verdurer,[62]
and early in the 14th century Alan, the son of Richard, and
John de Billesburgh held in this township two bovates of land
from the king, by payment of 6d. annually,[63] and a John, son

---

[58] *Lanc. Inquisitions,* Chet. Soc. vol. xcv, p. 16.
[59] *Lancashire Survey,* 1320-1346, Chet. Soc. lxxiv, p. 51.
[60] *Plac de Quo Warranto,* pp. 373-379.   [61] *Inq Post. Mort.*
[62] Baines' *Lanc.* vol. i, p. 251, first edition.
[63] *Testa de Nevill,* fol. 404.

of Richard de Billesburgh had granted to him (about the same period) an acre of land by the Abbot of Cockersand.[64]   Another early owner of the soil here was Elena, wife of Roger Brockholes, who died 8th December 31 Edw. III (1357).[65]

Richard de Balderston held the manor of Billesburgh from the Prior of St. John of Jerusalem by service of 12*d.* per annum, and died seised of it 20th December 1456, his son and heir being William de Balderston, then being aged 29.[66]

Richard Barton of Barton Row, who died 25th October 1572, held three houses and forty acres of land in this township in socage from Henry Cottam, gentleman, and the yearly clear value thereof was 6*s.*[67] (Cottam family see chapter vii).   Bilsborrow is now in the hands of many proprietors.

CABUS.

This township is probably not of any great antiquity, as we find no mention of it (by this name) earlier than 8 Hen. VIII (1516), when Margaret, the wife of Nicholas Rigmayden, died seised of certain lands here.   The Barony Court of Nether Wyresdale has for a long period been held in Cabus.

CATTERALL.

In the *Domesday Survey* this is described as Cathrehala, and consisted of two carucates of land, then in cultivation.

The first William de Lancastre by deed without date gave to Bernard Fily-Rufus two carucates of land in Halcath (afterwards called Haworth) and Catterall, which Richard Fitz-Swane, and Beatrice Fitz-Robert, and Michael Atheleston held by knight's service.[68]   Baines quotes a deed, also without date, but presumed to have been made in the time of King John (1199–1216), by which Robert the son of Bernard grants " To the hospital of St. John of Jerusalem the manse of St. John the Baptist super

[64] *Coucher Book of Cockersand,* as quoted by Baines.
[65] *Inq. Post Mort.*   [66] *Ibid.*   [67] *Ibid,* vol. xiii, No. 8.
[68] Kuerden's *MSS.* in the Herald's College, vol. iv, H 3; also *Testa de Nevill,* fol. 401.

Howorth, with the chapel of St. John the Baptist, with the
demesnes, viz. from the bridge of Hawayd, following the Wyre,
to the bridge which is over the Wyre near St. Helen's, and so
from the said bridge following the ditch which is near my
messuage in Catterall, and so from my messuage following the
ditch to the road from Prestone, and so across the road towards
Slireshalgh to the land which was Spareling's, and from
Spareling's land to the Wyre. And all the lands which are
comprised between these divisions, and six acres in the township of Catteral-upon-Keldit,[69] which were Alan Fitz-Ralph's,
and my mill at Catterall, besides two acres of land near the house
which was Richard de Ricihale, in Wetre, to make a market."[70]

Amongst the early possessors of the soil here were the
Catteralls and the Rigmaydens.

In the early part of the thirteenth century Richard de Catterall
held lands in "Katerale" and "Hawach" or "Howatte," and in
1397 Adam de Catterall held a third of the manor from Thomas
Rigmayden.

"Hawach, Hawet, Hulcath," and "Howatte," are names
applied to the same place in Catterall, and gave the name to
"Haworth Milne,"which is described in deed, dated 21st Oct. 1637.
(Catterall family, see chapter vii).

Marmaduke de Twenge, who died before the year 1318, held
in Catterall certain lands *in capite* from the king, which he
granted to his son, William de Twenge, for the term of his life.[71]

In November 1415 (on the Sunday next before the Feast of St.
Thomas the Martyr), Sir Richard de Hoghton, Knt., died seised
of four houses and twenty acres of land and meadow in "Hawet,"
in the "vil de Catterall," which he held of the king, by service and
payment of 2s. 6d. annually to the prior of St. John of Jerusalem.[72]

---

[69] By "Keldit" is possibly meant the "Calder."

[70] Baines gives no clue to where the deed is deposited. If this chapel existed it
was doubtless erected for use of the Order of St. John of Jerusalem, which had considerable possessions in Garstang.

[71] Dodsworth *MSS.*, vol. lxii, KKK, fol. 21.

[72] *Inq. Post Mort.*, Chet. Soc., vol. xcv, p. 147.

A portion of Caterall is detached and lies a few miles to the north, between Bleasdale and Barnacre.

(Catterall hall, see chapter vii).

CLAUGHTON.

This is the "Clactune" of *Domesday Book*, see p. 4, and which is now pronounced Clighton. The "vil de Claghton," in which were "Heyham" and "Duncunberg" (now known as Dandy Birks), is mentioned in the deed of confirmation of the endowment of Garstang church, which was executed about the year 1241, and by which the tithes of Claughton were given to the Vicar of Garstang (see chapter ii).

Ralph de Bethum in 39 Hen. III (1254–55), was seised of lands in Claghton,[73] which descended to another of the same name (probably his son), who, according to the *Survey* of 1320–46,[74] held with Thomas, son of Gilbert de Singleton, two carves of land here of the heir of Alice, Countess of Lincoln, by service of a fifth part of a knight's fee, paying yearly for Castleward, of Lancaster, 2s. 2d.

In 20 Edw. I (1291–92) the Prior of the Hospital of St. John of Jerusalem and the Abbot of Cockersand were cited to show by what authority they claimed[75] the judging of thieves, assize of bread and ale, &c., in Claughton. Edmund, the Earl of Lancaster, had lands here of annual value of 2s. 2d.

This township gave its name to a family which at a very early period were lords of the soil. In 15 Edw. I (1286) William de Clachton was one of the viriders in a forest assize held at Lancaster, and at about the same period Roger de Claghton is a witness to a deed conveying lands in Claghton from John, son of Gilbert de Mireschough, to Richard son of Walter, son of Ranuld de Bosco, the other witnesses being Henry le Boteler, John de Catterall, John le Tayleur, Robert de la Gosenargh,

73 *Inq. Post Mort.*   74 Chet. Soc. vol. lxxiv, p. 44.
75 *Plac. de Quo War.* pp. 373–379.

E

and Gilbert de Wythington.[76] Another deed without date (but executed before the end of the thirteenth century) conveys from ────── de Claghton to Roger de Claghton, a grant of a rent-charge on a certain field in Claghton; this is witnessed by Roger de Billesburgh, John de Stamford, and others.[77] About the same date John de Plesyngton made a grant of land here to Gilbert, son of Richard, son of Walter de Claghton,[78] and in 12 Edw. I (1283–84) John, another son of Richard, the son of Walter de Claghton, granted to his son Robert all his lands and tenements in Claghton.[79] Amongst the witnesses to this deed is John de Mirscogh, who in 18 Edw. I (1290) conveyed to John, son of Thomas, son of Richard de Claghton all his premises in Claghton, which he had of the gift of John de Mirscogh. This is witnessed by John le Tailler de Kirkland.[80]

In 18 Edw. II (1324–25) by deed dated at Garstang church, John, the son of Thomas de Stamford, granted certain hereditaments in the "vill de Claghton" to William de Tatham.[81]

In 28 Hen. VI (1449) one of the jurors summoned by the escheator to meet at Garstang on the death of Robert Laurence was John Claghton.

In 1340–41 the sum of two marks was returned by the assessors of the "*Nonarum Inquisitiones*" as the amount to which the township was to be taxed.

By deed dated at Garstang, the Friday next after the Feast of St. Mary Magdalen, 17 Edw. III (1343), Robert de Plesington granted to Edmund de Mirescogh and his heirs, all his lands in Claghton in Amounderness called "le Brustarecroft," and "le Brustaremeadow." This deed is witnessed by Robert de Culwenn, William de Hornby, John de Tayllour, Richard de Catterall, and John de Cotum de Billesburgh.[82]

In 39 Edw. III (1365–66) Cecile, the wife of Roger de Myres-chogh, leased to Laurence de Myreschogh, chaplain, for thirty-two years, all her lands in the "vill de Claghton."[83]

[76] Title deeds in possession of W. Fitzherbert Brockholes, Esq.
[77] *Ibid.*   [78] *Ibid.*   [79] *Ibid.*   [80] *Ibid.*   [81] *Ibid.*
[82] Dodsworth *MSS.* 142 PP, fol. 62.   [83] *Ibid* 142 PP, fol. 15.

By deed dated Wednesday after the Feast of St. John the Baptist, 21 Rich. II (1397), John de Lethum, chaplain, granted to Alan, the son of William de Warberton and Margaret his wife, who was the daughter of John de Botyller de Kirkeland, all his lands, &c. in "Claghton."

Of a place in Claughton called "Hecham" or "Hegham" we find several notices in deeds of the thirteenth century, and of a family bearing the same name. By deed without date, Alice de Heham granted to Walter de Tatham the third part of a field called Henrifield in Hecham; and early in the thirteenth century Candeley, son of Matilda, granted premises in Hecham to his son William—the witnesses being William de Bollot and Paulinus de Gairstang[85] (the latter was living in 1226-7).

In 16 Edw. II (1322-23), William de Southworth conveyed his premises in Higham in Claughton to Elizabeth his daughter.[86]

John de B'desey, by deed dated (Monday at the end of Easter) 29 Edw. III (1355), granted all his lands in Hegham in the "vil de Claghton" to Robert de Haldelegh[87]; and in 22 Ric. II (1398-9) William de Beselegh let to John de Inskip his lands in Hegham in Claghton in Amounderness at a rent of 28d. per annum.[88]

Two centuries later Jane Beesley died seised of lands here.[89] The connection of the Brockholes family with this township will be referred to more particularly in chapter vii. As early as 32 Edw. III (1358-9) Elena, the wife of Roger Brockholes, held lands here; and in 1421-22,[90] the then representative of the family, John de Brockholes, is described as "of Claughton."[91]

The following may be accepted as a complete list of the inhabitants of Claughton, who, in 1689, held rateable property.[92]

[85] Title Deeds in possession of Fitzherbert Brockhole, Esq.   [86] Ibid.
[87] Dodsworth MSS., 149 T, fol. 71.   [88] Ibid, 142 PP, fol. 15.
[89] Inq. Post Mort., 36 Eliz. (1593-4).   [90] Ibid.
[91] Thirty-third Report of Keeper of Public Records, p. 19.
[92] Original MSS. in the possession of Mr. John Whitehead of Rochdale.

" By the Com^s for putting in Execution an Act for a grant to their Majes' of an aid of twelve in the pound for one grant for the necessary defense of their realmes.   You are hereby appointed and required to be Collectors for the Townshipp of Claughton in the said County of all and eury the sumes of money in the Schedule or Assessm^t hereunto anexed mensoned.

" And with in sixe dayes after your receipt hereof you are hereby required to demande of all and euvry the seuvrell persons in the said schedule the seuvrall sumes answering to their respective names, so that if any persons find themselves agreived by the said assessm^t they may appeal to us or any two or more of the said Com^s at the Towns Hall in . . . . . on the Eleventh day of November instant.

" And you are hereby farther required that after such appeals as aforesaid shall be determined you doe forthwith collect all and euery the sums charged for personallties and offices as also one moiety or halfe of all and euery the said sums of money or such other sumes as shall be seuvrally charged or the respective persons at the determination of the said appeals and pay the said seuvrall sumes over into the hands of Mr. James Roscow Head Collector for the Hundred of Amounderness at the house of Mr. Richard Woods in Preston on the twentie second day of this instant Novemb^r

" And in case any person shall neglect or refuse to pay.his or her rate or assessm^t charged by the said schedule you are forthwith after such demand to destrain upon any Messuage Lands or Tenem^t for which they stand charged or to distrain the person or persons so neglecting or refusing by his or their goods and chattells or with the assistance of your constable in the day time to break open any house chest, trunk or box where their goods are and the distress so taken to keep by the space of four days at the cost or charges of the owner thereof and if satisfaction be not made with in the space of four days, that you then cause the said distress to be apprized by two or three of the inhabitants of your said Township and cause the sale whereof to be made for payment of the sumes charged upon the defaulter rendring to the owner the overplus [if any be] all necessary charges in takeing and keeping the same being just deducted.   And further that you collect and leuy the other moiety or half of all and euery the said sumes of money charged for lands in like manner as aforesaid, so that you doe pay the same ouer unto Mr. James Roscow at the place aforesaid on the ffourteenth day of ffeb next and you are hereby authorized to retain in your hands three pence for enery twentie shillings by you so paid to the Head Collector, Recompense for your seruice.   Thereof fail not at your perills.

"Given under our hand and sealed at Garstang the ffourth day of Nouemb

"Anno R. R. et R^d Willi° et Marie Aug^e de primo Anogr.

L. RAWSTORNE

Dn^a 1689   CHR. PARKER[93]

To JOHN SALLOME   THO^s WINKLEY[94]

and JOHN BRADLOW   ROGER SUDER[95]

these   GE° ADDISON " [96]

Novemb the 2^d 1689   Assessm^t for the townshipp of Claughton by virtue of an Act of Parliament for a grant, &c., &c.

	£	s.	d.		£	s.	d.
Mr Richard Roa, Doct^r				Margaret Adamson			
of Diuinity[97]	01	02	00	widowe	00	02	00
John Brockholes Esqre.	01	04	00	Hugh Barton	00	02	00
Thomas Whitehead				Christopher Caton	00	01	00
Gent.	00	06	00	Thomas Whittingham...	00	04	00
Thomas Barton	00	04	00	Thomas Shephard	00	04	00
John Barton	00	06	00	Henry Herritage	00	04	00
George Bradshowe......	00	04	00	James Parkinson	00	01	00
Robert Wilson	00	03	00	William Walker	00	01	00
William Bomber.........	00	01	00	Benjamin Corney	00	01	00
James Morton	00	02	00	James Chippindale......	00	06	00
Anthony Walker.........	00	01	00	Anthony Walker	00	04	00
James Walker...........	00	01	00	John Sallom	00	04	00
Alice Walker widowe...	00	01	00	Thomas Caton	00	02	00
Robert Carter............	00	04	00	William Latus............	00	05	00
James Carter	00	05	00	Thomas Goose	00	01	00

93 Christopher Parker of Bradkirk, a Justice of the Peace.

94 Son of John Winckley of Preston, clerk ; he was Registrar of the Court of Chancery, Preston, and in 1679 served the office of Mayor.

95 Roger *Sudell* was Guild Mayor, Preston, in 1682.

96 George Addison was Mayor of Preston 1673.

97 The vicar, Dr. Wroe.

John Sallom	oo o1 oo	Elline Grason widowe...	oo o2 oo
John Brederton	oo o1 oo	Richard Shepard	oo o1 oo
John Chrichloe	oo o5 oo	Laurence Cottam	oo o8 oo
John Cartemill	oo o2 oo	Robert Maile or [? Moyle]	oo o2 oo
Robert Parkinson	oo o1 oo	Mary Bell widowe	oo o1 oo
William Grason	oo o5 oo	William Walmsley	oo o3 oo
Mrs Elline Sogg widowe	oo o4 oo	Thomas Wilkinson	
John Richardson	oo o4 oo	Gent	oo o5 oo
Richard Cortas	oo o2 oo	Thomas Caton	oo o1 oo
Robert Garner	oo o1 oo	Christopher Parkinson..	oo o1 oo
John Hall	oo o1 oo	Elizabeth Shepherd	
Thomas Hull	oo o2 oo	widowe	oo o1 oo
Elizabeth Arkwright	oo o3 oo	William Cartmell	oo o2 oo
Thomas Markwall	oo o2 oo	Richard Blackborne	oo o1 oo
Thomas Cardwell	oo o1 oo	ffrancis Clarkson	oo o2 oo
William Dowson	oo o1 oo		
John Allston	oo o4 oo	Sume totale...	o9 18 oo
Thomas ffrance	oo o2 oo		

wee return John Sallom ⎱ Collectors
and Joh. Bradloe ⎰ allowed by us L. Rawstorne.

CLEVELEY

is partly in Cockerham and partly in Garstang; there is little to record concerning it except that it formerly was part of the constablewick of Garstang, and still owes suit to the manor of Nether Wyresdale. We have not met with the name prior to 10 James I (1612–13) when a John Allen was declared to have died seised of lands in Cleveley.[99]

FORTON,

like the last township, is partly in Cockerham and partly in Garstang, and its northern extremity extends into the hundred of Lonsdale. At the time of the *Domesday Survey* only about 100 acres were named in "Fortune."

[99] *Inq. Post Mort.*

Before the foundation of Cockersand Abbey, the whole of Forton belonged to Warin de Lancastre, who in the early part of the reign of Hen. II (probably about 1160) granted to Aldred, the son of Hugo, half of "ffortun," at a rental of 111s. per annum.   Some forty years later Henry de Lancastre,[100] the son of Warin, living in 1199, granted certain lands here to the Abbot of Cockersand ; and about the same time Adam de Lee (who was one of the house of Lancastre) released what he held from Aldred de Forton, in half of Forton, to the abbey.   Richard, the son of Huan de fforton, Randulf de fforton, William de Nateby, John de Slathwaiteued, Adam the son of Swain de Kayballes, Jordanus Gosnar, and Thomas de Likebert, all conveyed lands, messuages, &c., in Forton, to the abbey, by deeds without date, but which doubtless were executed in the thirteenth century.[101] The monastery was further enriched by the following grants, viz. : from Jordan Gosnar four acres of land and a house in Forton, in 1333 ; from Henry Corlews, the son of Robert Corlews, by deed dated 1st April 6 Hen. V (1418) all his lands, messuages, and tenements in fforton, in the "vill" of Gairestang ; from John Calfson, 2nd Jan. 7 Edw. IV (1468) half an acre of land called Slathuaytehed in fforton, in Garstang ; from John Brekedaunte, 22nd Feb. 19 Hen. VII, 1504 (see p. 13), a close of land in fforton called the "ffall," in the holding of James Dawson.[102]

The above-named grants, and the rental of Cockersand (see p. 13), furnish conclusive evidence that towards the close of the fifteenth century nearly the whole of the township belonged to the abbey.   On 31st May 1490, Sir James Lawrence, Knt., died seized of lands in the manor of Forton, which descended to his son Thomas Lawrence.[103]

[100] Henry, the son of Warin de Lancastre, also granted certain rights of "pannage" in the "vill de fforton" to the Abbot of Furness (Dodsworth *MSS.* 90, fol. 107).

[101] Deeds were ordered by statute to be dated about 1290–1300.

[102] The various grants above named will be found in full, Chet. Soc. vol. lvii, p. 34, *et seq.*   The original deeds are in the possession of Mr. Whitehead, of Forton Hall.

[103] *Inq. Post Mort.*

Upon the dissolution of the monasteries, the manor of Forton was granted by Hen. VIII (by letters patent) to Thomas Holt of Gristlehurst,[104] who was knighted by Edward Earl of Hertford, in Scotland, 36 Hen. VIII (1544–45) and whose descendants held it for four generations. Theophilus Holt, the son of Thomas Holt (who was grandson of Sir Thomas) died seised of it; his *Inq. Post Mort.* was held 4 Chas. I (1628–29). In 19 Chas. I (1643–44) Richard Newsham of Forton, gentleman, John Corles of Ellell, yeoman, John ffox and James Clifton of Forton, yeomen, purchased the manor of Forton, with all its appurtenances, "for the use of themselves and the rest of the tenants" of the said manor, and they subsequently released to each tenant his share on his paying his proportion of the purchase money, thus by deed dated 6th Angust 1667 they conveyed to William Webster of Forton, yeoman, for the consideration of 8*l.* 15*s.* 0*d.* "all that messuage and tenement in fforton consisting of three acres of land" then in their possession, and for which the ancient rent was 6*s.* a year, excepting thereout one acre of land called "ffarsid," which William Webster had conveyed to Randle Taylor of Stodday, yeoman.[105] In the eighteenth century Forton Hall was held by Elizabeth, wife of Thomas Whitehead of Claughton, who executed a deed of gift conveying it to her younger son Thomas, whose decendants still hold it (see chapter vii).

HOLLETH.

A part of this very small township is in the parish of Cocker-ham ; the whole owes suit to the manor of Nether Wyresdale.

In 1516 "Hollock" is described as part of the manor of "Wodeacre" and was held by Thomas Rigmayden of the queen as of her Duchy of Lancaster,[106] and it was retained by his

---

[104] *Cal. to Plead.*

[105] Deed in possession of Mr. Whitehead of Forton. The other tenants were treated with in the same manner.

[106] *Inq. Post Mort.* 8 Hen. VIII and 30 Eliz.

descendant, Walter Rigmayden, in 1588, and subsequently passed to one of the Dukes of Hamilton. The principal land owner now is Richard Cardwell Gardner, Esq.

KIRKLAND (Churchtown).[107]

In this township stands the parish church which is a mile and a half from the town of Garstang. The cluster of houses near the church is known as Garstang Churchtown.

Kirkland doubtless derives its name, either from its having been the original endowment of the church, or from the church being erected there; if the former, then at an early date some portion of the estate must have been alienated, as in the confirmation deed of 1241 (see chapter ii) provision is only made for the vicar of Garstang to have free right of common in the woodlands of Kirkland, with a moiety of the tithes of pannage of Kirkland, an oxgang of land and two houses; the remainder of the township being held by William de Lancastre, who, by deed without date, but which must have been executed in or near the year 1242, gave certain of his lands in Kirkland to Robert de Tayllour and his heirs for ever; a year or two afterwards he granted to the same certain other lands there, with the right of fishing in the waters, great and small, in his domain of Wyresdale.[108]

William de Lancastre, however, at the time of his death (*Inq. Post Mort.* dated 31 Hen. III, 1246–7) was seised of the manor of "Kirkelond."

By grant dated at Garstang, on Sunday next before the Nativity of our Lord, 13 Edw. I (1284), William, the son of Alan

---

[107] Toward the commencement of last century, locally Kirkland appears to have been called Churchtown, which name it still remains; it was designated Kirktown as early as 1600 (see chapter iv, Vicar Aynesworth); and in 1712 we find "Garstang Kirktown" (see chapter iv, Vicar H. Richmond).

[108] Dodsworth *MSS.*, vol. lxii KKK, fol. 89.

F

de Cathirton, quit claimed John, the son of Robert de Tayllour de Kirkland, and his heirs, of the right of pannage for forty pigs in the woods of Kirkland.[109]

Between 1277 and 1285, the abbot of Cockersand entered into an agreement with one John de Kirkland respecting an acre of land and dead wood in the wood of Kirkland.[110]

By deed dated at Garstang the day after the Feast of the Annunciation of our Lady, 23 Edw. III (26 March 1349), William Balderston, the parson of St. Michael's-on-the-Wyre, John de Plesington and John de Brockholes, conveyed to John le Taillour and Margaret his wife, the manor of Kirkland with its appurtenances, which, after their decease, was to descend to William de Kirklond and his heirs male, failing such issue, then to John, his brother, with remainder to his other brothers, Nicholas, Laurence and Robert, and in case none of them had male issue, then to revert to the right heirs of the said William de Kirklond.[111] This deed was witnessed by Richard de Kighley, Nicholas le Boteler, John de Barton, Knt., Robert de Plessington, John de Rigmayden, Richard de Caterhall, and others.

Notwithstanding the above named grants the lords of the fee were the descendants of William de Lancastre; and William de Coucy, second son of Ingelram de Gynes (see p. 6), and Robert de Coucy de Gynes held possession in 20 Edw. III (1346-7).[112]

The *Inq. Post Mort.* taken at Preston, on the Saturday next after the Feast of St. John before the Latin Gate, 36 Edw. III (1362), upon the death of William de Kirkeland furnishes the following conclusive evidence on the point.

William de Kirkeland died on Wednesday, the Feast of the Conception of the Blessed Virgin, 35 Edw. III (8th Dec. 1361), and then held only one messuage and sixty acres of land in Kirke-

[109] *Ibid*, fol. 90. This John le Tayllour de Kirkland was a witness to a deed dated 18 Edw. I (1290).

[110] Dodsworth *MSS.;* vol. lxii KKK, fol. 90. This deed is witnessed by Henry de Lee, *tunc. viccœm de Lanc.;* he was high sheriff in 1277 and 1284-5.

[111] Dodsworth *MSS.*, vol. lxii KKK, fol. 90.

[112] *Inq. Post Mort.*

land, of the annual value of 60s.; all the rest of his lands here he
had assigned to Roger de Gosenargh, William de Eccleston, and
Ralph de Knoll, chaplains, to the intent that after his decease
they should grant the same to Margaret his wife for the term of
her life, and after her death to Alice his daughter, and her heirs
male ; failing such issue then to her sister Joan, with remainder
in like manner to her younger sister Katherine ; but in default of
male issue then to the heirs of him the said William de Kirkeland.[113]   The lands so assigned were held of the moiety of the
manor of Wyresdale, which formerly belonged to William de
Coucy, and were then in the holding of John de Coupeland, by
commission of the king, by service of 1d. or half pound of
cummin in socage yearly for all services.[114]

An *Inq. Post Mort.* upon the death of Joan the wife of John
de Coupeland, Knt., was taken at Lancaster, on Monday, the
morrow of the Holy Trinity, 49 Edw. III (1375), from which it
appears that John le Botiller and Alice his wife held the manor
of Kirkland of Joan de Coupeland as of the hereditaments of
the said Alice, by homage and fealty, and the service of 10s. per
annum.[115]   It may be assumed that John de Botiller had
married Alice the daughter of William de Kirkeland, and that
subsequently the manor became the freehold of the Butlers of
Kirkland, whose descendants still hold it. (See Kirkland Hall,
chapter vii).

A branch of the Kirkland family was settled in Derbyshire
for several centuries, and bore arms.[116]

---

[113] William de Kirkland was possibly the third son of Sir William de Kirkland of
Bampton, in the county of Derby, Knt., whose ancestors, for several generations, were
lords of Kirkland in Cumberland, but proof is wanted. Sir William married Matilda,
sister to Alan de Coupland, and daughter of Richard de Coupland (*MSS.* in possession
of Walter Kirkland, Esq., of Eastbourne).

[114] *Inq. Post Mort.*   Record Office, 36 Edw. III, No. 102.

[115] *Ibid.*   Record Office, 49 Edw. III, No. 29.

[116] See *Genealogies of the families of Bate and Kirkland,* compiled by J. Paul
Rylands, F.S.A.   Privately printed, 1877.

ARMS.   Sable, three mullets Argent, within a bordure en-
engrailed Or.

CREST.   On a ducal coronet Or, a falcon proper, jessed and
belled, Gold.

NATEBY.

Notwithstanding the Danish termination "bye" or "bi" signi-
fying a dwelling place or habitation, we find no trace of this
township until the time of William de Lancastre, who, in the
reign of Henry III, granted to Hugo Northman and his heirs,
one bovate of land[117] in Natebi, for which he was to pay annually
2*d.* at Easter and 2*d.* at the Feast of St. Michael.   Amongst the
witnesses to this deed was Henry le Facuner.[118]

Nateby was at this time, and for some period afterwards, held
in fee by the Lancastre family as part of the manor of Wyres-

[117] A "bovate" is variously estimated at from eight to twenty-four acres.
[118] Dodsworth *MSS.*, vol. cxlix T, fo. 77.

dale ; and before the close of the thirteenth century, a great part
of it was held by Ralph de Nateby and Lawrence Travers, who
probably paid rent or service to the chief lord. According to
the evidence supposed to have been furnished by William Travers
of Nateby, who lived 1563–1627, it appears that, by a deed
(then existing and marked D, but without date), Ralph Nateby
of Nateby had issue two sons, Thomas and William, the elder
of whom (Thomas) being about to enter "into religion," gave all
his lands in Nateby and Garstang to his younger brother ; about
the same time, Lawrence, the son and heir of Lawrence Travers
of Tulket, *armiger* (who was warden of the hospital of the
Blessed Mary Magdalen, at Preston), also being wishful to
"enter into a religious lyfe" did give "all his tytill in ye manor
of Nateby" to Thomas Travers, his younger brother, and to
Isabel, the daughter of William, the son of Ralph de Nateby,
and for the "better assurance of ye s^d manor and lands of Nateby
a ffyne was acknowledged att Lancaster by Nateby to Travers,"
20 Edward I (1291–92).[119]   It is scarcely necessary to add that
Thomas Travers and Isabel Nateby were afterwards married,
and from them descended the Travers of Nateby (see Nateby
Hall, chapter vii), who lived here until the middle of the seventeenth century.

In 20 Edward III (1346–47) John de Kirkland, John de
Plesington, and Richard de Caterall, state upon oath [120] that
John de Plesington held of William de Coucy and Robert Coucy
de Guynes (see chapter vii) a bovate of land in Magna Nateby,
by knight's service, and that Robert de Plesington and Robert
de Bower held of the same, and by the same service, a bovate of
land in Magna Nateby.

On 23 May 1349, John Travers, the son of Thomas Travers of
Nateby, married Alice, the daughter of Robert Plesington, who
probably had for her dower the land just referred to (Bower
House, see chapter vii).

---

[119] *Ibid*, vol. lxxix O, fo. 39.
[120] *Inq. Post Mort.*

PILLING.

The earliest mention of Pilling is contained in a grant from
Theobald Walter, made between the years 1193 and 1199, of
which the following is a translation : [121]

"Know all men present and future that J. T. Walt. for the divine
protection and for the love of the Blessed Mary for the Salvation of the
soul of King Henry [II] and of the soul of King Richard his son and
the soul of John Earl of Moreton [afterwards King John] and of the
soul of Randle de Glanvile dear to us and for the salvation of the soul
H. [Hubert][122] Archbishop of Canterbury our Brother and of Herveus
Walter my Father and of Matild' Walter my mother and for the salvation of my soul and [of the souls] of all my friends and benefactors and
ancessors and successors,— have given and conceded and by this my
charter have confirmed all my Haye of Pylin to God and the blessed
Mary and the Abbot and Canons of the Præmonstracensian order there
serving God, in clear and pepetual Alms for the building[123] of one
abbacy of that order. Wherefore I will and order that the aforesaid
abbot and canons there serving God have and hold the said Haye freely
with all its appurtenances and the messuages pertaining to it free and
quit and absolved from all secular exaction and service from payment
of foresters and from all other cause as freely as alms can be given in a
free Haye, in wood or plain, in meadow and pasture in waters in pools
in fish-ponds in mills in fisheries in saltpits in marshes both moist and
dry and in all liberties and easements of the aforesaid Haye, both those
which now are and those which may thence arise

"Witnessed: Will' Poer. Benedict Gernet, Ralph de Bethum, Roger
his brother, Gilbert de Kentewelle Hubert bastard, Roger de Leicester,
Robert de Brun Warin Banastre, T. his brother William the son of
Martin, Helias the son of Roger, Adam de Kellet, Adam son of Heseb'
William de Winequic Geoffry de Barton William de Heston, Richard
his brother, Walter de Slopisb' [Shrewsbury]."

---

[121] Baines's *Lanc.*, second edition, vol. ii, p. 435; and Whitaker's *History of
Richmondshire*.

[122] Hubert was elected archbishop 1193, and died 13 July 1205.

[123] In Baines's translation the word "there" is here inserted; it is not in the original.

The *Haye* or *Haiæ* was a name applied to portions of the forest which were enclosed with a hedge, and into which beasts were driven, either for capture or slaughter; in some parts of England, at the present day, the word *haye* is used to express a fence or hedge (see Nether Wyresdale).

From this grant of Theobald Walter's it appears that the Abbey of Cockersand was not then built, although license to build it had been obtained from the mother house at Leicester some years before, and been confirmed by Pope Clement in 1190,[124] who, at the same time, ordered that it should be called the Monastery of St. Mary of the Præmonstratensian Order of Cockersand.

In the face of this, it is not quite clear what is meant by the allusions to the "Abbot and Canons *there* (*i.e.*, in Pilling) serving God," unless we suppose that prior to the erection of the monastery there was a temporary establishment at Pilling.

In 2 John (1200–01) the pasture of Pilling was confirmed to the abbey,[125] yet in 1292 Edward I. called upon the Abbot of Cockersand to show by what right he claimed the judging of thieves, assize of bread and ale, &c., in Pilling, when evidence upon oath was given which satisfied the jury that the grant made by King John was a valid one, and that it included all the wastes of Pilling, and that the abbatial lands in Pilling were exempt from all fines and amercements.[126]

In the time of Henry III the forests of Lancaster were given to Edmund Crouchback, Earl of Lancaster; and in 15 Edward I a forest assize was held at Lancaster on the Monday after Easter day (1286), when Adam de Carlton, Roger the son of Roger of middle Routheclyve, and Richard his brother, were charged with having killed three stags in the moss of Pelyn, which was part of the royal forest[127] (of Wyresdale). At this assize, amongst the

---

[124] Baines's *Hist. of Lancashire.*
[125] *Rot. Chart.*, M 8, No. 26.
[126] *Placit de Quo. War.*, 20 Edward I, Rot. 7.
[127] *Carta de Foresta*, Record Office (see Baines's *Lanc.*, first edition, vol. i, p. 250).

"Viridors" or "Verdurers"—who were officials sworn to receive
and enrol all presentments of trespasses against the forest laws
—were the following members of Garstang families, viz., Adam
de Brokholes heir of Roger de Brokholes, Thomas Travers,
John Gentyl, Roger de Wedacre, John de Ryggemayden, Roger
de Bylesbury, William de Clachton.

From shortly after this time to the dissolution of the monasteries a large portion of Pilling belonged to the abbey (see
Pilling Hall, chapter vii). A small part of the township belongs
to Cockerham parish. Formerly a large track of land in the
western part of the district consisted of peaty land, called
Pilling Moss (see page 2), which furnished turf in such quantities
as to give rise to the saying, "as inexhaustible as Pilling Moss,"
much of this has now become cultivated land, but the dike-like
fences characterise the township, as they did when the ballad of
Flodden Field was written

<blockquote>
"They wth ye Standley howte forthe went
From Pemberton and Pillin Dikes" [128]
</blockquote>

The following description of the sudden uplifting of Pilling
Moss is from the pen of the Rev. Legh Richmond, at that time
vicar of Garstang.

A copy of a letter from the Rev. Mr. Richmond, to —— Leigh,
   Esq., of Adlington, in the county of Chester, concerning a
   moving moss in the neighbourhood of Church-Town, in
   Lancashire. Communicated by Edward Milward, M.D.,
   F.R.S. [read February 28, 1744-45].

" Dear Sir

      As you will probably hear that this neighbourhood is greatly
alarmed with what they call a miracle, it may not be unacceptable if I
give you the History of it.

   " On Saturday the 26th of Jan. 1744-5 a part of Pilling Moss lying
between Hescomb Houses and an estate of Mr. Butler's called Wild

<hr>

[128] *Harl. MSS.*, Cod. 3526.

Bear was observed to rise to a surprising height; after a short time it sunk as much below the Level and moved slowly toward the South side, in half an hour's time it cover'd 20 acres of land. The improved land adjoining that part of the Moss which moves is a concave circle containing near 100 acres which is well nigh fill'd up with Moss and Water. In some parts it is thought to be five yards deep. A family is driven out of their dwelling house which is quite surrounded and the fabric tumbling down. Mr. Butler, Whitehead and Stephen White are the first sufferers by this uncommon accident. An intense frost retards the regress of the Moss to day, but I fear it will yet spoil a great deal of land. The part of the Moss which is sunk like the bed of a River runs North and South, is above a mile in length and near half a mile in breadth so that I apprehend there will be a continued current to the South. A man was going over the Moss when it began to move, as he was going Eastward he perceived to his great astonishment that the ground under his feet moved Southward.

"He turned back speedily and had the good fortune to escape being swallowed up. I have been at the Moss to make observations every day this week.

"If any thing happens worth your knowledge you may depend upon hearing from

Sir

Your very affectionate

Humble Servant

L. Richmond."

WINMARLEIGH.

A Gregorie de Winnerlie or de Wimerlegh, in the reign of Henry III, is said to have granted to the Abbot of Cockersand a portion of his lands near the lands of William Fitz Hervy, mentioning amongst other boundaries an oak signed with a cross.[129]

---

[129] Baines gives as his authority for this *Regist. S. Maria de Lanc. MSS.*, fo. 3 *bis*; but *Harl. MSS.*, 3764, which contains this register, furnishes no such record, but it does mention the final agreement (also quoted by Baines) between Gregory de Wim'legh and Geoffrey, the Prior of Lancaster, concerning six bovates of land in Hull.

A deed without date, but of the time of William de Lancastre, is witnessed by Gregory de Wynmerleigh and Roger his son, and about the same time appears the name of Hugh de Winmerley.[130]   An agreement, made between the Abbot of Cockersand and John de Kirkeland, is witnessed by Henry de Lee, High Sheriff of Lancashire, and John de Wynmerley.[131]

In 1343 (17 Edward III) Robert de Plesington received a fine from Thomas le Gentyll, Katherine his wife, and Ranulf their son, for half the manor of Wynmeles,[132] and in 20 Edw. III (1346–47) Thomas le Gentyll died seized of two bovates of land in Wynmerle. By deed dated at Wynmerlegh, on Monday next after the Epiphany, 12 Edward III (1339), Thomas, the son of William de Gentill, gave John de Haverington 129 acres, a waste which he held in Wynmerlegh in the "vil" of Garstange.[133]

In 34 Edward III (1360–61) a fine for a writ of Formeden,[134] concerning the manor of Wynmerley, was issued for Nicholas le Gentill, who was probably the son of Thomas le Gentill.[135]

At this time part of the land of Winmarleigh was held of the manor of Wyresdale, and some of this land was in the possession of William, the son of William le Molyneux (cousin and heir of Richard), whose *Inq. Post Mort.* was dated 36 Edward III (1362–63); and probably the land of which John de Travers was seized in 36 Edward III (1362–3) was of the same holding.

About the year 1365 the king gave into the custody of James de Pickeringe, Knt., all the lands and tenements of which Sir Thomas de Havrington had died seized (*Inq. Post Mort.*, 38 Edward III) in Winmarlegh, which were not held of the manor of Wyersdale,[136] which lands had descended to him from

---

[130] Dodsworth *MSS.*, vol. liii H, ff. 182 and 162.

[131] John de Lee held the office in 1277 and 1284-5.

[132] Bag of Pedes Finium, Chapter house, Westminster.

[133] Dodsworth *MSS.*, vol. cxlvii S, fo. 40.

[134] Writ of Formeden is in the nature of a writ of right which lies for him who holds lands by virtue of an entail.

[135] *Thirty-second Report of Deputy Keeper of Public Records*, p. 346.

[136] Dodsworth *MSS.*, vol. lxxxiv P, fo. 143, one messuage and forty acres of land.

his father, Sir John de Havrington de Farleton, who held them in right of his wife.[137]

About this time a Roger de Wynmerlegh had half the manor, and Christiana, one of his daughters and heiresses, married Henry de Rowall,[138] and Isabella, the other daughter, it is presumed (the evidence is not of a positive nature), married Henry de Plesington. By deed dated at Winmarleigh, Wednesday next after the Feast of the blessed Mary Magdalen, 3 Hen. VI (1425), Thomas Henryson de Rowall, heir of Christiana, daughter and heiress of Roger de Wynmerleigh, and late wife of Henry de Rowall, gave to Christopher, his brother, half the manor of Wynmerlegh in the "vil" of Garstange,[139] and by another deed dated 1 October 12 Edw. IV (1472), John Rigmayden, the son and heir of John Rigmayden deceased, quit claimed Ralph Radcliff, Hugh Radcliff and Richard Radcliff of all right or title in the whole of the lands and tenements in Wynmerlegh which he had received from Christopher Rowall which were of the inheritance of Henry Rowall, ancestor of Christopher Rowall.[140] A John Rowall had a tenement here from the abbot of Cockersand in 1451 [141] (see page 10). As before stated, Isabella de Rowall married Henry de Plesington, and Isabella, their daughter and heiress, having married Richard de Radcliffe, the whole manor subsequently passed to that family, and was held by them for many generations, until William Radcliffe [142] died, 1561, without surviving issue, when Winmarleigh passed to his sister Ann, daughter of Thomas Radcliffe, who had married Sir Gilbert Gerard, Knt., who was Attorney-General in 1567 and Master of the Rolls.[143]

---

[137] John de Havrington held lands in Winmarleigh.
[138] Dodsworth *MSS.*, vol. cliii, fo. 89.
[139] *Ibid*, vol. cliii WW, fo. 155.   [140] *Ibid*, fo. 47.
[141] The Abbey had several tenants of this name here in 1451 and 1501, see p. 9, *et seq.*
[142] A complete pedigree of the Radcliffes of Winmarleigh is given in Whitaker's *Whalley*, fourth edition, vol. ii, p. 81, compiled by Mr. W. Langton; it is therefore unnecessary to reprint it.
[143] Herald Visitations, &c., see pedigree.

The estates then passed in succession to their son Thomas, who afterwards became lord Gerard, to their grandson Gilbert, second lord Gerard, and ultimately to Dutton, third lord Gerard, who had issue by his first wife, lady Mary Fane, daughter of Francis, earl of Westmorland, a son and heir, Charles, fourth lord Gerard; the Winmarleigh property did not, however, pass to him, but to the honourable Elizabeth Gerard, who was the only issue of Dutton lord Gerard, by his second marriage in 1636 (with lady Elizabeth O'Bryan, daughter of Henry earl of Thornond), and who married the honourable William Spencer, third son of William, second baron Spencer, who was living at Ashton hall in 1664. The honourable William Spencer and Elizabeth his wife had issue a son William Spencer, who, by Mary his wife, left issue two sons, John and Charles, and a daughter Elizabeth, who married Robert Hesketh, Esq., of Rufford, and whose only daughter and heiress married, in 1714, Sir Edward Stanley, Bart., afterwards eleventh earl of Derby. William Spencer the younger had also a daughter Alice, who married the Rev. Harry Style, and survived her brothers John and Charles, and was thus the last representative of the Spencer family.

As an illustration of the tenure of land here at this period, we quote the following from an indenture dated 12 October 1668, between "the Hon. William Spencer of Ashton hall, in the county of Lancaster, Esq., and the Hon. Elizabeth his wife on the one part and ffrancis Deyes of Cockerham yeoman on the other," which witnesseth that the said William Spencer and Elizabeth his wife have granted and "to farme letten to the said ffrances Deyes all that their messuage &c. lying in Winmerleigh called by the name of Townend Tenement," late in the occupation of the said ffrancis Deyes, at the yearly rent of 31s. 4d. To have and to hold, &c., for 99 years, if Arthur Deyes, ffrancis Deyes, and Robert Deyes, three children of the said ffrancis Deyes, if any of them shall happen so long to live, paying in addition to the said rent, after the death of any tenant, their best live beast, in the name of a Herriott, and "also one good

rent or boone Cock and 5 rent or boone Henns yearly [144] at the
Feast of the Nativity of our Lord God," and also " keeping one
Hound or Spaniell," and to do " two days plowing in the time of
Corne seeding and four days shereinge or reepinge of Corne with
an able Reaper in the time of Corne Harvest yearly, and two
days harrowinge with an able harrowe yearly and also doing
suit and service of Court from tyme to tyme to be held of the
mannor of Winmerleigh, and also grinding of all the Corne and
Grain yearly growing upon the said premises at the Milne of the
said William Spencer in Winmerleigh aforesaid."

The Winmarleigh estate was sold in 1743 to pay off lady
Derby's portion, and conveyed by deed bearing date 18 and 19
March 1744,[145] to Thomas Patten, Esq., from whom it descended
to the right honourable John Wilson Patten, M.P., who was
elevated to the peerage in 1874 as lord Winmarleigh, and to
whom the entire township now belongs.

NETHER WYRESDALE.

At the completion of the *Domesday Survey* (A.D. 1086), Wyresdale was included in the land described as being "waste," *i.e.*, in
its wild or uncultivated state ; but sometime within the next
century a colony of Cistercian Monks from Furness had a
temporary settlement there, but about A.D. 1188 they removed to
Ireland, where they founded an abbey.[146] In 1102 the lands in
Amounderness, held by Roger de Poicton, which doubtless
included Wyresdale, became the property of the crown, and in
1245 we find that William de Lancastre granted to Robert
le Taylour liberty of free fishing in all the waters, great and
small, in his manor of " Wiresdale,"[147]   Richard I. had, how-

---

[144] The custom of paying a *boon* cock, hen or capon, is of great antiquity, see
page 9.   The indenture appeared in the *Manchester Courier, Local Gleanings*, July
1876.

[145] Title Deeds, &c., kindly furnished by James Nicholson, Esq., F.S.A.

[146] Dugdale's *Monas.*

[147] Dodsworth *M.S.S.*, vol. lxii KKK, fo. 89.

ever, given the royal prerogatives in the forests of Lancashire
to his brother John, Earl of Morton, who, in the first year of
his reign (1199–1200), confirmed a charter, whereby he granted
to the knights, thanes and freeholders of the county, the privileges
of cutting, selling, and giving their forest wood at their will without being subject to the forest regulations ; and also to hunt and
take hares, foxes, rabbits, and all kinds of wild beast, except stag,
hind, and roebuck, and wild hogs, in all parts of the forest, except
in the "demesne hayas." [148]

In the perambulation of the forests of Lancashire in
12 Henry III (1227–28) Wyresdale is not named, but by charter
dated at St. Paul's, London, 30 June 1266, Henry III granted to
Edmund, his son (Edmund Crouchback), inter alia, "all his vaccary
and forest of Wiresdale.[149]

In the time of Edward II, Thomas Thwenge was forester of
Wyresdale, and in 22 Edward IV (1482), there were two foresters
of Wyresdale who were each paid annually 30s. 4d.;[150] and in or
about 1588 the "maister of Wiresdale and Quernmore were paid
3l. os. 8d. a year," and it is declared that amongst the forests,
chases, and parks belonging to the duchy, out of which the
Chancellor, Attorney General, Receiver General, and two
Auditors, are to have deer, summer and winter, was Wiresdale.[151] Leland, in the time of Henry VIII, describes Wyresdale
as a deer forest, "partly woody and partly hethye."

The manor of Wyresdale, in the time of William de Lancastre,
probably included what are now known as Over and Nether
Wyresdale, the latter only forming part of the parish of Garstang.

In 18 Edward III (1344–5) Robert de Guynes held half the
manor of Wyresdale[152] (which John de Plesington held it of him
by knight's service), and which afterwards descended to John,

---

[148] Duchy Records Rot., fo. 12.
[149] The deed quoted in full in Baines's *Lanc.*, vol. i, p. 125, first edition.
[150] *Harl. MSS.*, codex. ccccxxxiii, fo. 317a.
[151] *MSS.* heading of Duchy Fees, &c. (Baines's *Lanc.*, vol. i, p. 48, second edition).
[152] *Inq. Post Mort.*, 20 Edward III.

Duke of Bedford (see page 6), who died seized of it *in capite* of the crown by knight's service in 14 Henry VI (1435–6).[153]

The other moiety, in 16 Edward II (1322–3), was held by John, the son of John Rygmayden,[154] and continued in the holding of the same family for upwards of two centuries, when it was settled by John Rigmayden upon Anne, the daughter of Edward Tyldesley, who was about to marry his son and heir, Walter Rigmayden — the deed bears date 4 December 1573[155] (see chapter vii).

The administrators of Walter Rigmayden, in 1602, sold his interest in Garstang manor, and doubtless at the same time disposed of the moiety of Wyersdale to Thomas, Lord Gerard, who, in 1604, had become possessed of the entirety.[156]

The following Schedule furnishes the names and holding of every tenant in the township in 1604 and 1605 :

> A Schedule of all the tenntz wthin the Manno^r of Netherwiresdale wth there severall rentz and porc'ons of comon allotted them accordinge to certein Ar'les made betwene the right ho the lord Gerard and his tennte of the said Manno^r by Robte Dalton John Calvert Esq^{rs} & Mathew Dickenson gen Commission's in that behalfe appointed

Barnacre township

Thomas Blackburne	xxxij^s iiij^d	xvj acres
Edward Parkinson	xxvij^s	xiij acr' di
Oliver Cottam	xiij^s viij^d	vj acr' di
John Lee	xii^s iij^d	vi acr'
Henry Walker	xvj^s i^d	viij acr'
Richard Calvert	xvj^s iiij^d	viij
Thomas Bee	xij^s ij^d	vi acr'
John Reesley	xvij^s ij^d	viij acr' di

[153] *Inq. Post Mort.*, 20 Edward III.
[154] Dodsworth *MSS.*, vol. cxlix T, fo. 74. [155] *Inq. Post Mort.*
[156] Perhaps he had one half from his father, who may have held it in right of his wife, who was a daughter of Thomas Radcliffe of Winmarleigh.

David Holland	xjˢ	... v ac' di
Robte Tomlinson	viijˢ ijᵈ	... iiij ac'
John Dunderdale	vˢ iiijᵈ	... ij ac' di
Robte Edgford	vijˢ xjᵈ	... iiij ac'
Thomas Myrscoe	xxiiijˢ	... xii ac'
Robte Goose	xiiijˢ ijᵈ	... vij ac'
Myles Mercer	viijˢ vjᵈ	... iiij ac'
Alexander Goose	xxiijˢ	... xj ac' di
Richard Dunderdale	xxiˢ xjᵈ	... xj ac'
Henry Goose	xjˢ xᵈ	... vj ac'
John Parkinson	ijˢ ijᵈ	... j acr'
Richard P'kinson	xvijˢ xjᵈ	... viij acr' di
John Richardson	xvijˢ ixᵈ	... ix acr'
James Carter	xiiijˢ iijᵈ	... vij acr'
Cristofer Caton	xiiij vᵈ	... vij acr'
Vx John Bee	xjˢ	... v acr' di
John Lea	vjˢ viijᵈ	... iij acr'
Willᵐ Bailton	xiˢ vjᵈ	... v acr' di
James Puteson	xiiijˢ ijᵈ	... vij acr'
Gregory Stursacre & Anne Hodgson	xvjˢ	... viij acr
James Anderton esqʳ	xlˢ ijᵈ	... xx acr'
Richard Whittingham	xxiiijˢ	... xij acr

Bounds township

John Sydgreaves	viijˢ ijᵈ	... iiij acr'
Robte Edgford	vijˢ xᵈ	... iiij acr'
Willᵐ Cartmell	ixˢ xᵈ	... v acr'
John Cartmell	vjˢ iijᵈ	... iij acr'
Willᵐ Plesington	viijˢ iiijᵈ	... vi acr' di
Robᵗᵉ Bell	ixˢ	... iiij acr di
James Clarke	xxiˢ jᵈ	... x acr' di
Richard Cartmell	iiijˢ	... i acr' di
Richard Horsfall	xiijˢ iiijᵈ	... v acr' di
Richard Goose	iijˢ iijᵈ	... j acr'

Wyresdale quarter

John P'kinson of Dolfynholme	xxxˢ	... xv acr'
Willᵐ Parkinson of Nicksonhouse	xˢ vjᵈ	... v acr'
Cicelie Cathorne	xiˢ iijᵈ	... v acr di

Thomas Webster	xi^s iij^d	... v acr' di
John Harrison	xi^s iij^d	... v acr' di
Willm Burne	xi^s iij^d	... v acr' di
James Bruer	xij^s iiij^d	... vj acr'
Nicholas Burne	vij^s	... iij acr' di
Henry lee	v^s iiij^d ob.	... ij acr' di
Edmund Wynder of Marrybolds ...	v^s iiij^d ob.	... ij acr' di
John Wynder	xv^s x^d	... vij acr' di
James Clarke for Symkinson house.	iiij^s	... i acr' di
Richard Bruer	vij^s iiij^d	... iij acr' di
Willm Sykes	xvij^s	... viij acr' di
Willm Banes	xix^s vj^d	... ix^{en} acr' di
Thomas Potter	xj^s iii^d	... v acr' di
Thomas Wynder	viij^s	... iiij acr'
Vx J. Foxe	xij^s	... vj acr'
Willm Banes Jun'	x^s ix^d	... v acr'
John Webster	xviij^s i^d	... ix^{en} acr'
Thomas Stursacre	iiij^s iiij^d	... i acr' di
Richard Atkinson	xx^s ij^d	... x^{en} acr'
Anthony Pye	xvij^s v^d	... viij acr' di
Willm Langton of P'kehead	x^s viij^d	... v acr'
James Foxe	xiij^s viij^d	... v acr' di
Robte Foxe	xij^s iiij^d	... vj acr'
John Atkinson	vj viij^d	... iij acr'
Anthony Harrison for Blesard house	xv^s	... vij acr' di
John Myrscoe	xxvj^s viij^d	... xiij^{en} acr'
Richard Corles	xxij^s viij^d	... xj^{en} acr'
Anthony Eltis	xiij^s iiij^d	... vj acr' di
Robte Wyndres	xvij^s	... viij^t acr' di
John Williamson	xx^s iij^d	... x^{en} acr'
John Caton	xij^s ij^d	... vi acr'
Edmund Wynder	xiiij^s	... vij acr'
John Brade	vij^s	... iij acr' di
Henry Lee	xv^s ij^d	... vij acr' di
Robte Webster	vj^s	... iij acr'
Henry Pickringe	x^s	... v acr'
Willm Wildinge	x^s	... v acr'
Rob^{te} Banes	vj^s j^d	... iij acr'

H

John Bee	xiiij^s	... vii acr'
John Myrscoe Junr	xiiij^s	... vij acr'
Robte Kytchin	x^s	... v acr'
John Rigmayden	xij^s v^d	... vj acr'
Richard lea	vij^s iiij^d	... iij acr' di
Edward Hodgson	iiij^s	... ij acr'
Ux Thome Walton	vj^s i^d	... iij acr'
Antho Foxe	viij^s v^d	... iiij acr'
Oliver Gardner	vj^s xj^d	... iij acr' di
Thomas Byrches	x^s ij^d	... v acr'
Thomas Bradeley	x^s ··^{d}	... v acr'
Willm Cartmell	xiiij^s	... vij acr'
Richard Birches Jun	iiij^s j^d	... ij acr'
Willm Anderton	xj ij^d	... v acr'

Cleveley

Anthony Gardiner	xij^s j^d	... vj acr'
John Holden	xxviij^s ij^d	... xiiij acr'
Thomas Fox	ij^s vj^d	... j acr'
John Myller a†s Atkinson	vij viij^d	... iij acr' di
John Walker	xviij x^d	... ix^{en} acr'
Margaret Townson	vj^s viij^d	... iij acr'
Cristofer Kempe	ix^s iiij^d	... iiij acr' di
Oliver Gardiner	xiiij x^d	... vij acr'
Willm Langton	xxj^s	... x^{en} acr' di
Edward Ashburner	v^s	... ij acr' di
Cristofer Cawson	xvj^s viij^d	... viij^t acr'
Phillip Calvert	xv^s v^d	... vij acr' di
Ux Gardiner	xix^s	... ix^{en} acr' di
John Atkinson a†s Myller	vj^d viij^d	... iij acr'
Vx Willi Fox	vj^d	... di acr'
John P'kinson	xij^s vj^d	... vj acr'

Hollorth

Ralph Harrison	xxxiij iiij^d	... xvj^{en} acr' di
Thomas Helme	xxxiij^s iiij^d	... xvj^{en} acr' di
Thomas Bond	xv^s	... vij acr' di
John Mason	iij^s	... j acr' di

Margaret Brade	vj^s viij^d	... iij acr'
John Bee	xiiij^s	... vij acr'
Jennett Brade.........................	vj viij	... iij acr'
Willm Clarke	xx^d	... j acr'
Willm Bee and James Hodgson ...	xviij^s	... ix^{en} acr'
Thomas Harrison	vij^s	... iij acr' di
John Parkinson	v^s vj^d	... ij acr' di
Anne Sykes	v^s	... ij acr' di
James Bulshawe	vij^s	... iij acr' di

Oxboad

Richard Celes	xxj^s vj^d	... x^{en} acr' di
Edward Curwen	xij^s iiij^d	... ij acr'
Anthony Ellis........................	xij^s iiij^d	... vj acr' di
John Curwen Junr	xiij^s vj^d	... vj acr' di
John Charnocke	xv^s	... vij ac' di
Willm Cerles	v^s ij^d	... ij acr' di
Robte Fowler........................	xviij^s iij^d	... ix^{en} acr'
Robte Garvis	v^s	... ij acr' di
John Carre	xix^s	... ix acr' di
Thomas Corles	vj^s x^d	... iij acr'
Robte Symkinson	vj^s viij^d	... iij acr'
Cristofer Curteis	ij^s vij^d	... j acr'
Nicholas Clarkson....................	xij^s	... vj acr'
Cristofer Walker.....................	xxij^s vj^d	... xj^{en} acr'
Thomas Syxe	iiij^s ij	... ij acr'
Richard Brade	xj^s iiij^d	... v acr' di
Roger Cartmell	ij^s iiij^d	... j acr'
Frauncis Best........................	vij^s vj^d	... iij acr' di
Richard Byrches	viij^s	... iiij acr'
Thomas Reeder......................	v^s	... ij acr' di
Willm Duderton	xxij^s	... xj^{en} acr'
Robte Robinson	xxv^s	... xij acr di'
Oliver Brade	xiiij^s	... vij acr'
John Corles	xv^s vj^d	... vij acr' di
Willm Corles	xv^s vj^d	... vij acr' di
Oliver Charnocke	xvj viij	... viij acr'
Thomas Charnocke	xv^s x^d	... vij acr' di

James Curwen of Hollins .... ij$_s$ j^d ... j acr'
Willm Fowler .... xiij^s v^d ... vj acr' di
John Curwen Sen .... xiij^s iiij^d ... vj acr' di

Longe More [*i.e.*, Pilling Moss]
Richard Parkinson.................... vij$_s$ ij^d ... iij acr' di
Robte Fowler.......................... vij^s ij^d ... iij acr' di
Robte Tomlinson .... xxij^s iiij^d ... xj^{en} acr' di
Thomas Curwen....................... vij^s viij^d ... iij acr' di

Remayninge of the thousand acres not devided or allotted to the tennt℮ aforesaid towards the satisfieinge of the Cottagers wthin the said Mannor of Netherwiresdale & the Charterers there the some of xxi acr' di.

The names of such tennt℮ as have accepted there severall porc'ons to them allotted & intended after the rate aforesaid (some more some lesse) at and before the Sixt daie of Marche Anno 1604 at a gen'all assemblie of the said tennt℮

James Atkinson .... i acr'
Thomas Jarvis .... v acr'
William Fisher .... j acr'
John Hubberstie .... ij acr' xx fall
Nicholas Tomlinson .... iij acr' vij fall
Robte Tomlinson .... v acr'
Thomas Curwen .... v acr'
Richard Parkinson.................... iiij acr'
Robte Fowler.......................... iij acr' di
James Chippengdale .... ij acr'
Thomas Bell .... v acr'
James Clarke .. .. xxiiij acr'
Richard Greene .... vij acr'
John Carre ... . iij acr'
Willm Langton .... xij acr'
Anthony Gardener.................... ij acr'
John Cartmell ... . i acr'
Anthonie Ellis .... vj acr'
Willm Anderton .... xvj acr'

Frauncis Best	x^n ac'
Thomas Sykes	iij acr'
James Curwen	viij^t acr'
Thomas Reeder	vj acr'
Christofer Walker	vj acr'
John Charnocke	vij acr'
John Curwen	xiij acr'
Edward Curwen	ij acr'
Oliver Charnocke	ij acr'
Thomas Charnocke	ij acr' i rode
Cristofer Curtees	j acr' i rode
Willm Rigmanden	ij acr'
Willm Fowler	ij acr'
John Cartmell	ij acr'
James Hey	i acr'
Oliver Brade	ij acr' j rode vj fall
John lee	viij^t acr'
Oliver Cottam	iiij acr'
Richard Dunderdale	iiij acr'
Thomas Blackborne	iij acr' i rode iij fa'
Richard Whittingham	iiij acr' i rode xv fall
John Rigmanden gen	x^{en} acr'
John Caton	ij acr'

The names of such tennt̸ as have consented to
the said Arłes at or before the said second of Aprill
& not heretofore by vs certified wth there severall de-
maunds of Comon &c.

Robte Plesington gen'	xij acr'
Richard Calvert	iiij acr'
Robte Goose	v acr'
James Pateson	v acr'
Gregory Stursacre	ij acr'
Nicholas Sidgreaves	iij acr'
Rob'te Bell of Calder and Richard Goose }	iij acr'
Willm Langton of P'kehead	v acr'
John Holden	o

John Walker	o
Margarett Townson	o
Willm Corles Junᵗ	ij acr'
Thomas Corles	di acr'
Richard Brade	ij acr'
Richard Birches	ij acr' di
Richard Corles	v acr'
Thomas Curwen	j acr'
Cristofer Curteis	j acr' i roode
John Charnocke	vij acr'

Robᵗ Dalton
Jo Calverley
Mat Dikenson[157]

Wyersdale passed from the Gerard family to the Dukes of Hamilton and Brandon (see p. 16), and in 1853 was sold, with Cabus and Cleveley, to the late Peter Ormerod of Wyersdale Park, Esq., whose widow is the present owner.

Baines, writing in 1836, refers to "a Saxon polity more ancient than the *Domesday Survey* existing in the *Constablewick* of Garstang until a recent period"; if there was at that time any authentic record of such a "Saxon polity" it is greatly to be regretted that it was not quoted by the author of *The History of Lancashire*, who only extracts a few lines from the "books of the court," which do not, in any way, prove that such an institution as a "Constablewick" ever existed in the parish.

The entry quoted is as follows: "June 29 1642. Ordered by the Court Jury, that the Court shall be yearly elected out of the several townships: the first year out of Barnacre, Bonds and Tarnican being thought a third part: the second out of Cabus, Cleveley and Holleth: and the third or remainder out of Wyersdale, Longmore or Pillin Moss and the other parts."

In the preceding pages the following facts have been recorded, viz., that in 1226 the township of Garstang was held by the Baron of Kendal and Wyersdale; in 1362 Sir John Haverington

---

[157] *Duchy Mis.*, Record E 65, A and B.

held lands in Garstang and Winmarleigh as of the manor of Wyersdale, whilst Barnacre-with-Bonds, Cabus, Cleveley, Holleth, Kirkland, and Nateby, all owed suit and service to the same manor ; and in the time of Edw. I. part of Pilling Moss belonged to the Forest of Wyersdale ; on the other hand we have no evidence whatever of any suit or service been paid to the manor of Garstang by any of the surrounding townships.

The fact is, the chief lordship or manor of the district was Wyersdale, and its lord held there a *Court Leet with a View of Frank Pledge*, from time immemorial, and does so at the present day, and the "Court Book" quoted by Baines (which is now lost or destroyed), doubtless referred to it, and not to Garstang, which only holds the court baron, which necessarily belong to every manor.

Baines whilst speaking of the "Constablewick of Garstang," admits that the court belonging to it met at Cabus under the direction of the Duke of Hamilton, the "superior Lord of the wick until 1816," whilst it is certain that long before this period the Hamilton family had ceased to have any interest in the manor of Garstang, whilst they retained the manorial rights of Nether Wyersdale until 1853.

There can be no doubt but that this court leet with view to Frank Pledge is of very great antiquity, and represents a relic of the old "Frith-borh or Peace Pledge," by which the "communitas" or inhabitants of the place were bound to each other, and to the State, for the maintenance of public peace. An ordinary court baron is not a court of record, but only regards the suit and service of the tenants of the lord, but the court leet is a court of record, and is held, not only on behalf of the lord, but also of the king.

From an old *MS.* volume belonging to this court[158] are taken the following particulars :

" PRECEPT to summon the court. You are hereby required to give due summons to the Court Leet with a view to Frank Pledge of our

---

[158] We are indebted to the present steward W. P. Fullagar, Esq., for the loan of this.

Sovereign Lord the King and Court Baron of Sir H. H [amilton] Bar^t Lord of the Manor afors^d to be holden at the house of   Inn Keeper in   afores^d on the   day of   at 10^{oth} clock aforenoon, that they be and personally appear at the day time and place above mentioned then and there to do and perform such suits and services as every of them respectively belong and wherewith they shall be charged and you are then and there to make return of due execution of the precept.

[159]W^m S[tyth] Steward

To ———— Warner for said Manor.   of the said Court."

The court was opened with the usual proclamation, calling upon all who had "suit and service" to answer to their names, those not so answering being returned as "defaulters," "essioned for" or "excused."[160] The old jury of thirteen, "good and lawful men of the manor," gave up their presentments, and a new jury was called and sworn, then followed the CHARGE, which, if read in full, must have sorely tried the patience of the court. The preamble sets forth that all "High Treasons, Petty Treasons and Felonys" are here "inquireable and presentable as the Leet is the King's Court, but not punishable"; and then follows a long list of crimes and their respective punishments, which it is not necessary to quote, as the details differ, but slightly, from those given *in extenso* in *The Manchester Court Leet Records* (Chetham Soc., vols. lxiii and lxv).

This is doubtless the charge which, in former times, was read on the elevated piece of ground now known as Constable Hillock. The jury next proceeded to enquire of the constables if they had "apprehended all vagabonds, rogues, and sturdy fellows"; if they had "pursued the hue and cry after theives and robbers"; if they kept the "stocks, ducking-stool, and shooting-butts in repairs"; and also, if the surveyors of highways, and overseers of the poor, had performed their duty.

---

[159] This William Styth is no doubt the Steward whose house was destroyed by fire in the middle of last century, but he was not as *Baines* states Steward of the manor of Garstang.

[160] Now the fine is 6*d.* for "essoign."

The jury are warned to enquire if the "comon pond" is looked after. The ale-house keepers, butchers,[161] bakers, &c., are to be watched; and all "forestallers, ingrossers, and regrators"[162] of corn and victuals presented.

From the records of the court held in 1822, it appears that the jury was elected as follows: two for Barnacre, one for Bonds, two for Cabus, one for Cleveley, one for Holleth, one for Pilling Moss, one for Tarnacre, and three for Wyersdale[163]; the following officers were also elected, viz., assessors, pinders, fence lookers, and house lookers, for the township of Barnacre-with-Bond, Cabus, Cleveley, Holleth, Nateby, and Wyersdale.

The court is still held annually (at the end of October) at the Hamilton Arms in Cabus, and although the "charge" is not read, most of the old customs are observed.

In Nether Wyersdale is the village of Scorton, which has been styled "the model village," because it contains neither a public-house, nor a doctor, nor a lawyer, nor a policeman. The scenery in the neighbourhood is fine, and in no way answers to the description of Wyersdale given by Camden, viz., "a solitary and dismal place." There are a few small mills in Wyersdale, which furnish employment to the inhabitants of Scorton and Dolphin-holme.

Scorton is a village of quite modern birth. John Rignayden, by will dated 20 October, 1587, bequeaths 30l. to Elizabeth Morrison "out of money yssuinge out of" his "farme of Scurton." (See Scorton Hall, chapter vii.)

THE TOWN OF GARSTANG.

In 20 Edward I. (1291-2) an unsuccessful attempt was made to prove that the Lord of Coucy was here holding a market, and

---

[161] Butchers are not to kill or sell the flesh of bulls "unbaited."

[162] Regrator is one who obtains by unfair means corn, &c., and sells the same in open market or fair. Ingrosser is one who gets corn, &c., by buying on promise, taking other than by demise, grant, or lease, &c., to the intent to sell again.

[163] The old jury was thirteen, see p. 56.

I

exercising various other rights which belonged exclusively to the crown (see p. 6). Edward II., by charter dated the fourth year of his reign (1310–11), granted to the Abbot of Cockersand the right to hold a market every Thursday at Garstang, and also a fair of two days duration, viz., on the vigil, and the day of the feast of the apostles St. Peter and St. Paul, *i.e.*, 28th and 29th June.[164] Baines in his *History of Lancashire*,[165] states that in the 7 Edward II. the town of Garstang was incorporated, but for this no authority has been found at the Record Office or elsewhere, and the subsequent history of the town renders it extremely improbable that such a charter was ever granted.

The right to hold a market and fair having been given to the Abbot of Cockersand, on the dissolution of that Monastery the privilege would lapse to the crown, and probably for the next half century no market or fair was held.

In the time of Henry VIII., Leland records in his itineray, "After I rode over Brok Water (he was journeying from Preston) rising a vi miles of in the hilles on the right hand and goeth at last into Wyre. Calder rising about the same hilles, goeth also into Wyre : I rode over hit.

"By the townes end of Garstange, I rode over a great stone bridge[166] on Wyer or I cam to it. Wyre rises a viii or tenne myles from Garstan out of the hilles on the right hande and cummeth by Greenhaugh a pretty castle of the lord of Darbys and more than half a myle thens to Garstang in Anderness.

"Sum saith that Garstang was a market towne."

What Leland meant by the last paragraph is, that at that time no market was held in Garstang, but that tradition said it had been a market town. This view is supported by the fact that on 13 January 1597, Queen Elizabeth granted "to the Inhabitants of the Towne of Garstange for the relief of the poore of the same Towne a weekely Market to be kept in the

---

[164] Rol. Chart, 4 Edward II.   [165] Vol. ii, p. 523, second edition.
[166] This old bridge was pulled down about the middle of the last century, and the present one erected.

same Towne upon the Stretewaie and also two Faires yearly the one upon the Feast daie of S⁺ Peter and Paul and the other upon S⁺ Martyn's daie in Wynter.[167]

Nearly a century later, a charter of incorporation was granted to the inhabitants of Garstang by Charles II.[168] The original Letter's Patent is in the custody of the present Bailiff. The following is an extract of a translation of it, taken from the Bailiff's Records.

" Charles the second by the grace of God &c &c. Whereas our Town of Garstang in our County of Lancaster is an ancient populous Town and whereas the inhabitants of the said town have humbly besought us that we would be graciously pleased to incorporate the said town by such name and to give and grant such liberties and priviliges to the Inhabitants thereof as to us should seem most expedient. . . . . We will by these presents for us our heirs &c so ordain and grant that the town of Garstang for ever hereafter may or shall be a Free Borough . . . . . and we make ordain and constitute Garstang a Free Borough and that the inhabitants thereof shall be a Body corporate by the name of the Bailiff and Burgesses of the Borough of Garstang . . . . and that they by the name of the Bailiff and Burgesses of the Borough of Garstang may and shall be for ever hereafter persons fit and capable in Law to have receive and possess any Manors, Lands &c to them and their successors for ever or for a term of years And also all Goods and chattels and every . . . . other matter or thing, and also to give grant demise alien 'assign' and dispose of such Manors Lands &c. . . . .

And that the Bailiff and Burgesses of the Borough aforesaid so appointed and their successors may for ever have a Common Seal for all manner of causes and business to be acted or done by them, and that it shall and may be lawful for the Bailiff and Burgesses of the Borough or their successors at their pleasure from time to time to break change and make new such seal. . . . . And further we Grant to the

---

[167] *State Papers* (Dom. Ser.), vol. ccxxxv, p. 4.

[168] An entry in the Bailiff's book states that an original charter from Edward II. was surrendered to Charles I., but as the writing is quite modern, it is probably merely an extract from Baines' *Hist. of Lanc.* The surrender merely referred to the market and fair.

said Bailiff and Burgesses that there shall and may be within the said
Borough one of the most honest and discreet men of the said Borough
to be elected and chosen in manner hereafter mentioned who shall be
and shall be called the Bailiff of the Borough And likewise that there
shall and may be seven sufficient and discreet men of the said Borough
to be elected in manner and form herein likewise aftermentioned who
shall be and shall be called the Burgesses of the said Borough out of
whom a Bailiff of the said Borough for the time being shall be elected
and for the better execution of the premises we have named assigned
constituted and made our trusty well beloved William Spencer the elder
Esquire to be the first and modern [present] Bailiff[169] of the said
Borough who shall take his Corporal Oath upon y*e* Holy Evangelist
before Thomas Butler Esquire rightly well and faithfully to execute the
said office and after such Oath so taken which said Oath we do give
and grant full power and authority to the said Thomas Butler to admini-
ster to the said William Spencer. We will and grant that he the said
William Spencer shall be and continue to be Bailiff and shall exercise
the said office until the Feast of S*t* Michael the Archangel which shall
be in the year 1680 and from the said Feast until another of the
Burgesses shall be elected and sworn Bailiff. And also we constitute
and make our well beloved subjects Ralph Longworth gentleman
Thomas Green Thomas Cooper Thomas Brewer and John Sturzaker
Inhabitants of the said Borough to be the seven first and modern
[present] Burgesses who shall every one of them take his corporall oath
upon the Holy Evangelist before the said modern [present] Bailiff rightly
well and faithfully to execute the office and every of them shall continue
a Burgess for and during their natural lives unless in the meantime for
bad governing or ill behaviour or for not inhabiting and staying within
the said Borough they or any of them shall be thence removed. And
further grant that the said Bailiff and Burgesses shall have power and
authority from year to year for ever upon the 29th of September to
assemble and meet together in any convenient place within the said
Town and elect a fit man of the Burgesses who being so elected shall
be Bailiff and continue in office for one year [provision is made for
election of Bailiff or Burgess in the case of death]. And we give and

---

[169] In the original the words are "primum et modernum," which would be better
translated "first and present."

grant to the said Bailiff and Burgesses free and lawful power to have receive and take to them any Manors, Messuages, Lands &c within our kingdom or elsewhere within our dominions, so as such Manors &c to be had purchased or received do not exceed in all the clear yearly rent of 50*l*.   And further we will and by our abundant special grace and favour we have given to the aforesaid Bailiffs and Burgesses that they shall have, hold and keep within the Borough towards the sustenance . . . . and relief of the poor Inhabitants thereof a Market to be holden there upon the Thursday weekly and every week for ever, and also a fair to be kept yearly to begin upon the Vigil or Eve of St Peter and Paul the Apostles and continue two days viz the said eve the said Feast of St Peter and St Paul and also another Fair to be holden yearly on Vigil or Eve of St Martin the Bishop in Winter to continue for two days in the usual Market or Fair place and upon the several days heretofore kept and now to us surrendered which said surrender we have accepted together with the Court of Piepowder in the time of the several Fairs aforesaid and all manner of tolls piccage stallage profits whatsoever to such Market and Fairs

Wherefore we strictly charge and command that the said Bailiffs &c for ever may have hold and enjoy in the said Borough a Market and Fairs and Court of Piepowder &c &c.

In testimony whereof we have caused these Letters to be made patents dated at Westminster the fifth day of August in the 31st year of our Reign [A.D. 1680].

The only Municipal Records which have been preserved are contained in a thick folio volume, from which we have extracted the following items :[170]

LIST OF BAILIFFS FROM 1680 TO 1800.

1680 William Spencer Esq.	1686 Mr Thos Brewer.
1681 Mr Ralph Longworth.	1687 Mr Jno Sturzaker.
1682 Mr Richd Rivington.	1688 Mr Willm Spencer Esq.
1683 Mr Wm Belton.	1689 Mr Thos Crone.
1684 Mr Thos Green.	1690 Richard Spencer Esqr.
1685 Mr Thos Cooper.	1691 Mr Jno Gardner.

[170] The Bailiff and Burgesses kindly placed the volume in our hands for the purpose.

1692 Richard Longworth Esqr.[171]
1693 M^r Jn° Butler.
1694 M^r Jn° Gardner.
1695 M^r Jn° Sturzaker.
1696 Mr Thos Crone.
1697 M^r Jn° Catton.
1698 Richard Spencer Esq p' dup^y.
1699 Chas Sallom.
1700 Richd Longworth Esqr.
1701 Mr Thos Beesley.
1702 M^r Jn° Butler.
1703 Mr Jon^r Gardner.
1704 Mr Jon^r Gardner.
1705 Mr Nich^s Wilkinson.
1706 Mr Nich^s Wilkinson.
1707 Mr Wm Bridsworth.
1708 Mr Wm Bridsworth.
1709 Mr Chas Sallom.
1710 Mr Jon^r Gardner.
1711 Mr Henry Lucas.
1712 Mr Richd Wilkinson.
1713 M^r Jn° Sturzaker.
1714 M^r Jn° Hathornthwaite.
1715 M^r Jn° Bell.
1716 M^r Jn° Corles Junr.
1717 Mr Robt Mason.
1718 Mr Chas Sallom.
1719 Mr Jon^r Gardner.
1720 Mr Nich^s Wilkinson.
1721 M^r Jn° Sturzaker.
1722 Mr Hathorthwaite.
1723 M^r Jn° Bell.
1724 M^r Jn° Corles.

1725 Mr Robt Mason.
1726 Mr Chas Sallom.
1727 „　„　„
1728 M^r Jn° Corles Senr
1729 Mr Wm Gardner.
1730 Mr Wm Hodgson.
1731 M^r Jn° Crone.
1732 Mr Benjⁿ Crone.
1733 M^r Jn° Farnworth.
1734 M^r Jn° Bell.
1735 Mr Chas Sallom.
1736 Mr Rob Fowler.
1737 Mr Rich Gould.
1738 M^r Jn° Corles.
1739 Mr Wm Gardner.
1740 Mr Wm Hodgson.
1741 M^r Jn° Farnworth.
1742 M^r Jn° Bell.
1743 Mr Robt Fowler.
1744 Mr Wm Rawthmell.
1745 „　„　„
1746 Mr Eprahim Briggs.
1747 M^r Jn° Wallis.
1748 Mr Wm Gardner.
1749 Mr Thos Walker.
1750 M^r Jn° Styth.
1751 Mr Richd Lucas.
1752 Mr Thos Gardner.
1753 Mr Wm Walker.
1754 Mr Ch^r Rawlinson.
1755 M^r Jn° Burn.
1756 Mr Henry Lucas.
1757 M^r Jn° Styth.

[171] An Inscription on St. Thomas Chapel (see *post*) is said to have mentioned Richard Longworth, Bailiff, in 1666, and another Incription on the old Bell refers to "Balives" in 1668, but by what authority the office was held does not appear. Prior to this date we have not found any reference to a Bailiff.

1758 Mr Richd Lucas.
1759 Mr Thos Gardner.
1760 Mr Thos Bell.
1761 Mr Jno Clarke.
1762 Mr Ch^r Rawlinson.
1763 Mr Jno Burn.
1764 Mr Henry Lucas.
1765 Mr Richd Lucas.
1766 Mr Thos Gardner.
1767 Mr Thos Bell.
1768 Mr Thos Bell.
1769 Mr Jno Coggan.
1770 Mr Thos Clarke.
1771 Mr Henry Lucas.
1772 Mr Thos Gardner.
1773 Mr Jno Guy.
1774 Mr Jno Bell.
1775 Mr Thos Bell.
1776 Mr Jno Coggan.
1777 Mr Thos Clarke.
1778 Mr Henry Lucas.
1779 Mr Thos Gardner.

1780 Mr Jno Guy.
1781 Mr Jno Brodbelt.
1782 Mr Jno Bell.
1783 Mr Jo^s Clarke Junr.
1784 Mr Webster Bell.
1785 Mr James Harrison.
1786 Mr Thos Gardner.
1787 Mr Jno Bell.
1788 Mr Jo^s Clarke Junr.
1789 Mr Andrew Blackburn.
1790 Mr Peter Bell.
1791 Mr Ja^s Carter.
1792 Mr Robt Clarke.
1793 Mr Thos Bell Junr.
1794 Mr Thos Bell.
1795 Mr Jno Bell.
1796 Mr Thos Clarke.
1797 Mr Peter Bell.
1798 Mr Thos Bell Junr.
1799 Mr James Carter.
1800 Mr Robt Henrie.[172]

After this list follows the oaths of the Burgesses, the Freemen, the Toll-man, and the Town Sergeant.

A record of the Freemen admitted since 1721 is next given, and amongst them are :—

Rev. Wm Bushell[173] Clerk.
    „ Thomas Heywood Clerk (Thos. Hayward vicar of Garstang).
    „ Thomas Parkinson Clerk.
Matthew Low Lieut. in 8th Reg.
Rob. Charnley gent de Wildbore House.
Rev. Wm Willowsey.
Tho. Whitehead gent.
Benj. Whitehead.

[172] The *MS.* list is complete to the present date.   [173] The curate of Goosnargh.

Edwd Crombleholme.
Rev. Wm Crombleholme[174] Jur 29 Sep. 1730.
Legh Richmond (The Vicar).
Evan Wall.
John Braidley sen.
Thos Lucas gen.
Alex. Butler Esq.
Joh Wakerfield of Bower House.
William Greenhalgh Esq.
Thos Sturzaker of London Victualler.
Jon^r Gardner of London Vintner.
Sylvester Richmond jun. gen.[175]
Byron Starkie gen.
Joshua Marshall gen. ens^n in Col. Clayton's Reg. of Foot.
Willm Hudleston Cur^te.
Antho^y Rigmaiden Jun, 21 Sep. 1738.
John Styth jun. 24 Nov. 1749.
Ja^s Pedder sworn 2 Nov. 1760.
Richd Crombleholme sworn 29 Sep. 1789.
Thos Lewtas Nateby Hall 1808 circa.
Geoffrey Hornby Rector of Winwick 30 Sep. 1811.
Thos Bell M.A. Junr Garstang late of.
Queen's Coll. Camb. sworn 4 Oct. 1825.

22 OCTOBER, 1717.

It is unanimously ordered and agreed that such Bailiff for the
Body Politick as shall hereafter be elected and chosen shall for
ever thereafter have liberty to expend the sum of ten shillings
yearly at the Assizes and Sessions of Peace, and shall have the
same allowed out of the Town's Stock, and no more.

The holding of the Courts since the year 1699 are regularly
recorded, and in one stereotyped form of words (in Latin), simply
setting forth that the last Bailiff has presented his accounts and

---

[174] The vicar of St. Michael's-on-Wyre.

[175] All the names before this are in one handwriting — afterwards the signatures or
"marks" of the Freeman appear.

that a new Bailiff is elected, and giving the names of the new Burgesses, of which the following examples will suffice :

BURGESSES.

1700	1720	
William Spencer Esq	Joh'es Sturzaker	gen.
Richard „ „	Nicūs Wilkinson	„
John Sturzaker Gen.	Joh'es Hathornthwᵗᵉ	„
Jonathan Gardner Gen.	Carolus Sallum	„
Chaˢ Sallom Gen.	Joh'es Bell	„
Thoˢ Crone Gen.	Rob'tus Mason	„
John Caton Gen.	Joh'es Corles	„

Mr Jonathan Gardner Deputy Bailliffe for Richard Spencer Esq his accounts of Receipts and Disbursements on the Towns accᵗ this last year given this 29ᵗʰ Sep 1699.

Receipts	£	s.	d.
In Tolles Recᵈ at Martinmas ffaire	01	08	08
Small Toll & Stallage	01	13	00
For Tolles at Peters ffaire	01	15	04
Small Tolls and Stallage....................................	01	12	00
Rent of Shopp, Towns Hall	01	10	00
ffor the Towns Hall..	00	08	00
	08	07	00

Disbursemᵗˢ	£	s.	d.
Spent at Martinmas ffaire	00	10	00
Att Peters ffaire	00	10	00
To tenn toll men for their Wages for four days attend-			
ance	02	00	00
Laid down for Assessⁿᵗˢ for yᵉ yeare	00	16	08
	3	16	8

K

29 SEPTEMBER, 1728.

	£ s. d.
Rec^d at Martmss ffaire in pickage and Stallage	04 02 02
„ in Stallage money the whole yeare	01 06 00
„ „ shop rent the whole yeare	01 10 00
„ „ Peters faire	03 12 02
„ „ Hodshon & Nicholas Brandle ye fine	01 00 00
„ „ towne Hall 2 Show men	00 05 00

Tott^l receipts   11 15 04

Disburst^m p^d the charge of the Election daye & when I was sworn Burgess	02 10 00
Given to the poore Inhabitants of Garstang in Beefe at Xissmtr.	01 00 00
p^d the towne Clerke his sallarye....................................	00 10 00
p^d the tolle mens wages at 2 faires	01 04 00
p^d expense & appeareing money at 2 assises.....................	00 12 00
p^d in .... to Sr Thomas Lowther[176].............................	00 10 00
p^d taxes repairs of the chappell and other paym^{ts} & Expenses on the towns acc^t as by pticulars	05 09 04

11 15 04

From the particulars of these accounts, which have in some cases been preserved, the following extracts are given :

RECEIPTS.

1702	Rec^d for Thos Sturzaker's ffreedom	00 06 08
1715	„ at Martimas ffair at the time of the Rebellion...	00 00 03
1737	„ Thomas Hamilton Esq. gift toward a new cloak for Sergeant	00 10 06
1737	„ Mr Sutton's gift towards a Bible [probably for the chapel]	01 10 00
1769	„ for the Italian Dwarf for the Town Hall	00 07 00

[176] Sir Thomas Lowther of Holker was elected M.P. for Lancaster in 1722, 1734, and 1741.

DISBURSMENTS.

1702	Att the Coronation Day	01 08 00
1703	„ a Bone fire	00 05 00
„	To the Serg^t a new Coate Breeches & makeinge	01 15 00
„	„ Wm Preston for Lead for the Cross	00 04 00
1714	for mend^g Rogues Post	00 01 04
„	Mr Moncaster Town Clerk his sallary	00 10 00
1716	Sp^t ab^t Scriveners	00 01 06
	Passengers	00 06 00
1724	Sp^t with Dragoon Officers	00 02 00
1725-6	Sp^t at severall Times in treating the Officers when billetted Soldiers	00 07 00
1730	Given to Poor Passengers and disbanded Soldiers and Sailors	00 13 00
1732	At visiting Dutchess Hamilton	00 05 00
„	Spent at severall times on the Clergy	00 13 00
1733	When Butter was weighed and assise of Bread	00 00 08
1734	Expended in treating the Dutchess of Hamilton	01 09 00
„	The like on Mr Richmond and other Clergymen	00 07 06
1735	Spent wth Mr Chorley who gave Pray^r Book	00 02 00
1741	On Admiral Vernons Birthday	00 02 06
„	„ Adm. Vernons taking Porto Bello	00 06 06
1742	Costs in Eject^t agt Whitehead etc.	00 11 02
„	Given to Soldiers Ale to go out of Town	00 00 06
1754	Spent for removing old Cross	00 01 08
1755	Paid for mending Halberts	0 0 8
1768	„ for a Sacrament Certificate	0 1 6

At the Fairs it appears that it was necessary for the vendor of horses to obtain a certificate, of which copies were entered in the town's book. The following are selected :

Januarie the 7th 1697.

Wiłł Richardson of Mirscow bought a Black Bay mare with a star on ye forehead & with a mealy mouth ye taile & maine black about thirteen years of age of Wiłł Browne of Burnsay in ye County of York.

ffor ye mare aboue mentioned I doe avouch to bee honestly & truely come to by ye above named Wiłł Browne as witness my hand

George Browne

23 June 1718.

Mr John . . . . . . of Garstang in the County of Lanc. then bought an Iron Gray colour'd Gelding wth a cloudy face ab^t fourteen hands & an half high comeinge six years old of John Robinson of Bpprick of Durham

ffor the Gelding above named we do joyntly & severally avouch to be honestly & truely come to by the above named John Robinson   Witness our hand

George Wilkinson
Robert Conden

In 1742 the local authorities managed to lose possession of their Town Hall, and an order was made for "an ejectment against Mr. Joseph Whitehead and Mr. Robert Browne" who had "kept possession without any permission of the Bailiff and Burgesses."

29 October 1789, the Bailiff and Burgesses did "name and appoint the Lyon Levant" to be their "common seal for all purposes whatsoever."   The seal is still in use.

On the 9th of February 1830, an additional fair was instituted to be held on 12th and 13th days of April for the sale of "meat, cattle, horses, sheep, pigs, wares, and merchandise."

Blome, in 1673, describes Garstang as "indifferent good town" which "hath a great market for corn, cattle, yarn and fish, on Thursdays";[177] and William Stout records that, in 1691, the market for cheese was "mostly at Garstang and Preston."[178]

---

[177] *Brit.*, p. 135.
[178] Autobiography of W. Stout, 1851.

Richard Brathwait, about the year 1650, published the first edition of his *Barnabee's Journal*, which contains the following incident :

> " Thence to Garstang pray you heark it,
> Ent'ring there a great beast market,
> As I jogged on the street
> T'was my fortune for to meet
> A young heifer, who before her
> Took me up and threw me o'er her."

After this it is not to be wondered at, that the traveller immediately departed for Preston.

The *Diary* of the Rev. Peter Walkden[179] furnishes a graphic description of a visit to this fair :

"Nov 11 (1729) So got ready for Garstang fair and having a design to offer my little mare for sale I set son Henry on her . . . . so we went direct to Garstang and put in our mares at Joseph Brown's and meeting Brother John Miller, I went with him and warmed me, and we had each a pint of ale.   He being gone I paid for both pints 4ᵈ, and I paid Joseph Brown for the half windle of barley that my son fetched. It would have been 7ˢ 4ᵈ had I given 3ˢ 8ᵈ a peck as I did for what I bought of him myself but he took 7ˢ and gave my Henry a penny.

"So I went and shewed my little mare and had 2 guineas bid for her, if I would bring her up to Mʳ Bolton's but I thought it too little.   So I stood most of the fair but had no more offer; so I put her into the croft and went down town and had a pint of ale with Richard Caiton at Willacee's.   Then went to have bought onions but found none to sell. I then bought 4 quarts of nuts at 2¼ᵈ, a pennyworth of gingerbread and a pair of gloves for son Henry.   So came to Joseph Brown's and set waiting for brother Miller and his brother Joseph Miller with whom I stayed while we had two pints of ale which brother Miller paid for ; so I got my mares and my son Henry, and went to brother Miller's to lodge."

Of the extent of this cattle fair at the commencement of the

---

[179] Extract from the *Diary* of the Rev. Peter Walkden, Preston, 1866, p. 66 (Peter Walkden was the non-conformist minister of Newton-in-Bowland and Hesketh Lane).

present century, an idea may be formed from the fact, that on the 22nd November 1805, no less than 3000 head of cattle passed through Lancaster to attend it.[180]

During the Civil War Garstang raised four companies for the Parliamentary army under the command of John Fyffe of Wedicar hall, Christopher White of Claughton, and Richard Whitehead of Garstang town (see Greenhalgh castle, p. 20).

During the rebellion of 1715 the inhabitants of Garstang were not all true to the reigning monarch, but contributed their quota to the rebel army. On the 9th November (1715), the insurgents left Lancaster *en route* for Preston, but finding the "day rainy and the ways deep they left the Foot at a small market-Town called Garstang, with orders to advance next morning to Preston, which they accordingly did."[181]

The only recruit whose name was recorded as having been induced to join the standard of the *Chevalier de St. George*, was Roger Monkcaster, an attorney-at-law and town clerk of the corporation.[182]

Roger Moncaster (or Muncaster) was not a native, and very little is known about him; on 29 May 1710, he was married at Church Town to Alice, daughter of Robert Plesington of Dimples, and he appears to have been on terms of intimacy with Thomas Tyldesley and other well-known supporters of the Pretender's cause. The Tyldesley *Diary* contains several allusions to him:

"1712 May 6. Thence to Garstange. Spent 6^d at Mrs Bessley's but Mr Muncaster treated us att Betty Wakeffeilds one:

"July 20. Spent 4^d at Bradley's in Garstang with Mr Plesington. Muncaster younge Morecroft ye lether officer and Will. Webster.

"1713 July 23. Went with cos. Butler to Nepy's [an inn] in Garstange Spent 6^d with Mr Moncast^r Jo. Wadsworth Tho. Barton and Jack Gleave."[183]

[180] *Lancaster Records*, p. 26.
[181] Patten's *History of the Rebellion*, p. 95.
[182] Clarke's *Journal*, see Chet. Soc., vol. v, p. 99.
[183] The Tyldesley *Diary*, edited by Joseph Gillow and A. Hewitson, 1873.

Muncaster followed the army to Preston, and being there taken prisoner was tried at the assizes on the 20th January following, convicted of high treason, and condemned to die the traitor's death; and accordingly, on the 27 January 1716, he and four others were executed at Gallows hill, Preston. Before his execution he handed to the sheriff the following declaration :

" Dear Friends
        " I am brought hither to be a Miserable and Dismal Spectator to you all. The crime I am accused of, condemned and brought hither to be executed for, bears no manner or less infamous Title than Rebellion, a Crime prohibited both by the Laws of God and Man, and tho' I be the Person, not the only person to suffer for it, yet I declare that from my heart I do detest and abhor the very principles of Rebellion, and look upon the promoters and abettors thereof to be men without any, or at least any good principles, and enemies, in the highest degree to the lawful Sovereign King George and Country. I shall not trouble you any further with this, but acquaint you, that upon a serious recollection of my bypast, and God knows too long continued transgressions and offences both against God and Man, and a strict view and inquiry to the outmost of my power into my wicked course of life, those very sins that I have wretchedly committed, have brought the deserved vengeance of God upon me, tho' they shelter and cloke themselves under the base title of my crime.
        " I heartily, and with the utmost sincerity, repent of my sins of what nature soever, and I hope through Faith, and the merits and intercession of my blessed Saviour and Redeemer to obtain remission thereof.
        " And I in perfect charity with all men, and freely from my heart, forgive all, particularly every one concerned in my Execution, desiring forgiveness of all persons, here present or elsewhere, whom I have anywise offended. I was educated in the Protestant Religion, of the Established Church of England, have continued so all my life, and dye in the same and am sorry that I should blemish the Church by my late proceedings, for which I now die, and beg patience to hear repeat the Articles of my Christian Faith. I believe &c. I desire you would take such caution from my unfortunate example, as may prevent the like to any of you. I desire you would all join with, and for me, in Prayer to Almighty God

for remission of my sins, and that through the merits and mediation of his Son Jesus Christ, our only Saviour and Redeemer, I may meet with a glorious resurrection to Life eternal." [184]

The town clerk was not, however, the only rebel in Garstang, for amongst the prisoners taken to London was John Leybourne of Nateby, and amongst those tried at Liverpool were Edward Sykes of Nether Wyersdale, labourer; Thomas Walmesley of Bilsborough, innkeeper; Joseph Wadsworth of Catterall, gentleman; Thomas Cartmel of Bilsborough, yeoman, and Thomas Goose, Junior, of Catterall. Of these the two first were acquitted, but the three last were condemned, and were executed at Garstang (tradition says at Stock Lane End, Catterall) on 14 February 1716, along with one Allan Sanderson, a ship carpenter of Preston. [185]

In the accounts of Thomas Crisp, Esq., high sheriff of Lancashire, appears the following item:

"Feb. 15-16, 1715-16. Charge at Garstang and Lancaster on executing 4 at either place 22*l.* 0*s.* 8*d.*, besides the undersheriffs."

Joseph Wadsworth was a son of Nicholas Wadsworth of Haighton, whose father, Hugh Wadsworth, recorded a pedigree in 1664-5 (see Dugdale's *Visitation*); like Roger Muncaster he was a "chum" of Thomas Tyldesley's, and his name often occurs in his diary, where he is termed "cos" (cousin), but in what way he was related does not appear.

"1712, May 6. Wee parted about 7: but att John Corley's door old cos Tom Goose, cos Wadsworth, Mr. Plesington, and young cos Tom Goose with Will. Bolton stayed us till 9. Wee spent 1*s.* each: and p^d pro young Tom Goose."

"June 5. Went early in the morning ffox hunting with cos Wadsworth to meet Mr. Penket and found a ffox, but could not holle him; afterwards went to Garstange."

"1713, Feb. 28. Cos Wadsworth dined and stayed all night."

[184] Clarke's *Preston Fight*, Chet. Soc., vol. v, p. 199.
[185] *Ibid.*

The "young Tom Goose" above named was no doubt the companion of Wadsworth on the scaffold ; a family of that name had, for several generations, been settled in the parish ; in 25 Eliz. (1582–3), a Thomas Gose is defendant in a case, brought before the Duchy Court, concerning lands called the "Wrazes" in Winmarleigh ;[186] in 1604, Alexander, Robert, and Henry Goose held lands in Barnacre under the Lord Gerard; and in 1641, Richard Goose of Catterall, Henry Goose of Wyersdale, Thomas and Henry Goose of Barnacre, John and James Goose of Claughton, were amongst those who had not taken the protestation (see *post*). A local tradition obtains that Goose was arrested at Garstang for shouting out to the rebels as he stood on market cross,

"Hey ye on me lads and you'll take the crown with a distaff."[187]

Nothing is known concerning Thomas Cartmell, except that he belonged to an old Garstang family, the name appearing in the Church Register in 1567, and several of the family being tenants of the Lord of Wyersdale in 1604 (see p. 48).

The Parish Registers record the burial, on 16 February 1715–16, of "Mr Joseph Wadsworth and Thos Goose of Catterall, and Thos Cartmell of Claughton, Rebells." [188]

In the Rebellion of 1745 the Rebel Army again passed through Garstang, arriving there on the 27 November on their way to Preston, and on the day following, James Ray the author of *A complete History of the Rebellion*, and a volunteer under his Royal Highness, the Duke of Cumberland, arrived there, and to use his own words, "I allighted at Capt. Gardner's at the Royal Oak.   At my first setting out to reconnoitre the Rebels, I proposed to pass and repass them, in the Road in the Station of a Trader, going about my own private affairs ; for which I was provided with bills of Parcels, Letters of Orders, &c., in case I should be searched by them, as it might more evidently appear

---

[186] *Cal. to Pleadings*, vol. iii, p. 149.
[187] Hewitson, *Our Country Churches*, p. 474.
[188] Cartmell is by Clarke described as of Bilsborough.

I was the real person pretended to be ; but being advised not to venture among them, by reason I might find it a great difficulty to acquit myself of them again, as they might be too penetrating to see through such a disguise. Seeing my desires could not be readily fulfilled in this way, I resolved to take some other method, which might be full as prejudicial as the former, viz., on taking up their straglers ; and being informed that there was two in the Town which happened to stay behind their Command, I resolved to go and take them : for which purpose I borrowed a Fuzee and a case of pistols, so being shewed to their Quarters, I immediately went in, and took them Prisoners, and after disarming them, with which arms I supply'd myself, committed them to the care of a Constable, who, with his guard, conducted them safe to Lancaster Castle. In the Road to Preston I picked up another stragler."

A tale is still told at Garstang that during the short stay of the Rebels here, their treasure box was stolen and secreted in a ditch in a field behind, and a little to the south of the Town Hall; but in consequence of the threats of the soldiers the money was restored.[189]

The parish of Garstang from Pilling to Nether Wyersdale extends fourteen miles, and from Cabus to Bilsborrow five miles, and comprises an area of over 28,800 statute acres. The river Wyre rises from two rivulets in Nether Wyersdale ; near Scorton it is joined by a stream called Grizedale Beck, at Catterall it is increased by the Calder (which rises in the Bleasdale hills) and just as it leaves the parish the Brock runs into it. The Broadfleet, a stream which springs out of the mosses on the west of the parish, discharges itself into a small arm of Morecambe bay at Pilling.

The population of Garstang was, until quite a recent date, entirely engaged in agriculture. In the early part of the present century extensive calico works were established by Messrs.

---

[189] Hewitson's *Our Country Churches*, p. 474.

Fielding, which were closed in 1830; since that time a few cotton and other mills have been erected.

Between 1861 and 1871 the population of the entire parish slightly decreased.

The following Table will show the area and population of the parish and the several townships:

	Area in Statute Acres as given on Ordnance Map.	Inhabited Houses in 1871.	Population 1861.	Population 1871.
Claughton	3785	111	608	526
Catterall	1741	142	867	672
Kirkland	974	71	388	336
Nateby	2086	67	385	435
Winmarleigh	2342	47	246	289
Cabus	1388	32	209	171
Garstang...........................	502	155	714	687
Barnacre-with-Bonds	4494	174	907	922
Nether Wyersdale	4214	109	667	549
Forton ....*	1279	127	574	549
Holleth ....*	358	†4	†30	35
Cleveley ....*	620	†8	†62	40
Bilsborrow	851	35	176	185
Pilling...........................	6060	260	1388	1572

* Includes the whole township — part of which only is in Garstang.
† In the parish of Garstang only.

CHAPTER II.

ECCLESIASTICAL HISTORY.

ALTHOUGH the *Domesday* survey does not furnish evidence
that a church at Garstang at that time existed, it would
not be safe to infer that it had not then been erected.   William
de Lancastre, who was steward to Henry II. (about a century
after the *Domesday* survey) held the church of Garstang, and
Warin de Lancastre, his son, granted all his right to the advowson of it to the abbot of Cockersand, before the close of the
twelfth century,[1] and in 17 John (1215–16), Gilbert, the son of
Roger, the son of Reinfrid, who had married Helewise, the
daughter of William de Lancastre, conveyed his right to the
patronage of Garstang church to the same monastery, " for the
salvation of the souls of king Henry, king Richard, and his own
son and that of Helewise his wife." [2]

The church of " St Helens, near the bridge over the Wyre," is
mentioned in a deed of gift to the hospital of St. John of Jerusalem,
made in the time of John (see p. 24).

The grant made by Henry, the son of Warin de Lancastre
(who was living in 1198–99), conveying certain rights in Forton
to the abbot of Furness (see p. 31 *note*), was witnessed by " Robert
the Parson of Gairstang."   Sometime during the reign of John
(1199–1216), William de Lancastre, the son of Henry de Lancastre, granted the advowson of the church of Garstang to the
abbot of Cockersand, with all its appurtenances ;[3] the grant

---

[1] Dugdale's *Monasticon* ; also Chet. Soc., vol. lvii, p. 34.
[2] Dodsworth *MSS.*, vol. liii, fol. 22.   *Rot. Chart.*, 17 John, *m* 4, *n* 24.
[3] Dodswosth *MSS.*, 149 T, 127.

being witnessed by (amongst others) Ralph de Betham, Richard de Coupeland, and Robert de Gairstange.

In 5 John (1203–4), Gilbert Fitz Reinfrid appeared as plaintiff and Magister Matthew (probably vicar of St. Michael) as defendant, the question to be decided being, did the church of Garstang belong to St. Michael's-upon-Wyre or not? The jury decided that "the church of St Helen of Geresteng never was a chapel belonging to the church of St Michael upon Wir which is in the king's gift but they have judged it to have been always in their times a mother church."[4]

The lost Coucher Book of Cockersand contained a confirmation of the rights of the abbot and convent to the advowson of the church of Garstang, of which fortunately a copy in the original Latin is preserved in Whitaker's *Richmondshire* (see appendix A), and a translation of it is amongst the church papers,[5] the text of which is as follows :

"To all Christian People &c. John Le Romaine Archdeacon of Richmond, send greeting, know ye that we out of our pious and charitable regard commiserating the poverty of the Abbot and Convent of Cockersand, since they had before a discreet and fully experienced authority committed to our administration of the Church of Garstang itself, and all things appertaining thereunto, have confirmed the same to them and their successors for ever, for the benefit of the poor and of strangers and the advantage of the same house.

"They are to bestow an unencumbered Vicarage upon us and our successors by presenting a Vicar to the same Vicarage, rated as follows. That is to say, that the vicar in the name of the Vicar, may have and receive for ever tithes of all kind, as well great as small, and increase of all kind of what denomination so ever throughout the whole village of Claughton, to which village Heyham and Duncunberg belong. And from the said Village, with its appurtenances the Vicar shall have all 'obventions and oblations both of the dead and living. The Vicar shall also

---

[4] Fragment Record. incert. temp. R. John Rot. 3 in dorso.

[5] A copy in Latin was, about 1758, in the possession of the Rev. James Pedder, on which was endorsed "the original of this is writ in an old character & very much abbreviated the Archdeacon's seal is at it."

have the free right of common, in the wood-lands of Garstang and Kirkland, with a moiety of the tithes of pannage of Kirkland.   Furthermore
the Vicar for the time being shall yearly have and receive for ever all
oblations of the parish church of Garstang, belonging to the three solemn
Feasts namely the Feast of the Nativity of our Saviour, of the Passover,
and of Mother Church, together with all the appointed dues, missals,
yearly records, masses for the dead, private benefits and other accustomed and small obventions due to the said Vicar, and his Chaplain on
account of Vigils, of Burials and of marriage.

"But let the said Vicar engage that he will faithfully perform all the
holy duties, which are to be performed in the Church of Garstang, and
that he will pay all the ordinary and accustomed Archideaconial dues
pertaining to the said Church.   The said Vicar shall yearly in the Vilage
above mentioned collect Peter's pence and the Archdeacon of the place
shall be responsible for them, according to his proportion in such manner as the Abbot and Covent shall be responsible for their proportions.
And be it known the Vicar shall have one sufficient mansion house near
the church yard, of the said church, which is called Philip-toft and shall
have one oxgang of ground within the limits of Garstang, with its appurtenances, exemption from payment of all tithes both great and small
and one dwelling house, with the aforesaid oxgang belonging to it, and
all other privileges and liberties to the same belonging, saving to us and
our successors, the wool and lamb and Peter's pence heretofore mentioned without any diminution throughout the whole Parish.

"In testimony whereof we have to these presents affixed our Seal."

The date of this confirmation must have been A.D. 1241, as John
le Romayn (who must not be confounded with the archbishop of
that name) was not archdeacon of Richmond until that year (he
died in 1256), and the confirmation itself was fortified by the
assent of Archbishop Walter Gray, with the Dean and Chapter
of York, and finally by a Bull of Pope Gregory IX., dated at the
Lateran, xiv kal. May, in the fifteenth[6] year of his pontificate
(A.D. 1241).

---

[6] Whitaker's *Richmondshire*, vol. ii, p. 449, where the last date is printed fifth year
of Gregory IX. (1232), a misprint for fifteenth year.   Walter Grey was bishop of
Worcester, and translated to York 1216, he died 1255.

In 30 Hen. III. (1244–6), Jordan, the son of Torfin, in consideration of 30s. quit claimed before the king's justices at Lancaster, to Henry, the abbot of Cockersand, one bovate and six acres of land, respecting which a suit had been instituted to try whether it was a "lay fee or an appurtenance to the rectory of Garstang."[7]

About the same date an agreement was made between the prior of Lancaster and the abbot of Cockersand respecting certain tithes, such agreement being necessary on account of the close proximity of Garstang to the Royal Forest where the abbot had exclusive rights (see appendix B).

Garstang church, according to the *Taxatio Ecclesiastica* of Pope Nicholas, A.D. 1291, was rated at 26l. 13s. 4d., the old tax being 10l.; the vicarage was 13l. 6s. 8d., and the old tax 5l.

The *Inquisitiones Nonarum*, which was completed in 1341, gives the following value, viz., ancient tax x marks, new tax xv marks, true value xx marks, of which Garstang pays xiiij marks, Claghton 2 marks, Catterall xxvi[s] viii[d], Bilsborough xx[s], the vicarage xx marks as ancient tax, and c[s] as new.

In 1357, Ellena, the wife of Roger de Brockholes, died seized of certain lands in Claughton, Billesburgh, and Catterall, which she held in socage of William de Tatham by service of one rose yearly, and to find a chaplain to celebrate divine service at Claughton, or in the church at Garstang, at a salary of 66s. 8d.[8]

The following confirmation of rights conveyed to the abbot of Cockersand by William de Lancastre is quoted by Whitaker as from the *Coucher Book* before named :

"Be hit knawen to all men y[t] whereas y[e] Abbot and Covent of Cockersond, are seisset and theyr p'decessores before theym of c'teyn Londez and tenementz, mesez, Rentz, Meddowes, Pasturez, Wastez, Mossez, Fysshyngez, Approwmentz made, and to be made and of oder dyuersez Possessionz, Franchez, and Prosetz and Esiamentz in the Towne of Gayrstang and Fforton by y[e] Gyft, Graunt and Feffement of S[r] William

---

[7] Whitaker's *Richmondshire* (appendix), quoting *Coucher Book* of Cockersand.
[8] *Inq. Post Mort.*, Record Office, 32 Edward III., No. 12.

Loncastre hold Lord of Wyersdale and of other dyuersez Senyours to holdt theym and theyr Successourez in pure and perpetuell Almons forev'more os theyre ryghte and y⁵ ryghte of theyr Kyrke of Seynt Elyn after y⁵ report of theyr munimentz to theyme y'ofe made and also by y⁵ v'tew of y⁵ same dedes to take vndrewod in y⁵ Wod of Wyresdale y⁵ is to sey hensbote and heybote and to delfe turves and carye at theyr wylle in y⁵ mosse of Gayrestang for theyme and theyr successours and theyr tenantz of Garstang as well for theym as y⁵ ere as for theym y⁵ ere to come.

" And open that Thomas Rygmayden Lord of y⁵ maner of Wedeacre by hys did y⁵ her is knawlagyng and affermant there ryght in forme as is aboueseyd in all poyntz wylls and grauntez for hym and hys heyers for ev'more y⁵ y⁵ abouesayd Abbot and Covent and theyr Successouris ne theyr tennantis of Gayrstang and Fforton ne be fro henseforthe by y⁵ seyd Thos. ne by hys heriez grevet molested empeched or desteurbed in noo poynt of thyng aboue wrytyn. And y⁵ they may peasable have and enjoye all theyr possessionz abouesey⁴ and doo theyr profetz and approwmentz in Fforton and in other Places w'in theyr Boundez and they and theyr tenantz take theyr Wod called estou's and delfe theyr turves in y⁵ mosses and turbarye in Gayrstang and theym carye and bere away at theyre wyll w'thout cont'adiction of hym or hys heyrs forev'more, as theyr ryght and as y⁵ ryght of theyr kyrke of Seynt Elyn. And all thes thynges well and trewly to hold and p'forme y⁵ sey⁴. Thes for hym and hys heyres to thys dede hase sett his seall.

" Gyffen at Gayrstang y⁵ Wedynnesday next after y⁵ Feaste of the Purific. of our Ladye in y⁵ yere of y⁵ reigne of Kynge Edward IIIᵈᵉ after y⁵ Conquest xxxvii^{th} " (1363).

In the beginning of the next century the church underwent some extensive repairs, as it appears that a warrant was issued in 4 Henry IV. (1402-3), to the chief foresters of Myerscough, to deliver to the parishioners of Garstang four timber oaks for the reparation of their parish church.

On the 24th February 1443-4, the archdeacon of Richmond issued a "monition" against the vicars of Lancaster and Garstang for non residence.[9]

---

[9] Regist. Arch. Richmond (Canon Raines' *Lanc. MSS.*, vol. xx, p. 372).

The *Valor Ecclesiasticus* (taken in 1535) furnishes the following details.   Under the head of "Spiritualities" belonging to the abbot of Cockersand, are:

	li.	s.	d.
Tithes of the Rectory of Garstang viz., of grain	xi	o	o
„ „ lambs and wool	v	o	o
„ „ calves	1	o	o
„ small &c., and Easter Dues	3	o	o
To the Vicar appertained a house with land worth per annum	o	11	o
Tithes of corn and grain...	8	13	4
„ „ lamb and wool..	1	13	4
„ small &c.	4	o	o
Total ...	14	17	8

From this was to be deducted Fees to the amount of 5*s.* 5*d.*

In 1725 Bishop Gastrell[10] records the Glebe was worth 20*l.*, Tithes 40*l.* 10*s.*, Easter and Surplice Dues 20*l.* or 25*l.* per annum.

By Will, dated 5 October 1554, Alys Radclyff of Thalleys' in Clitheroe, late wife of Thomas Radclyff of Winmerleigh, left "to the high awlter of Garstange iij[s] iiij[d]."[11]

The following is an inventory of "the Jowells, vestyments, ornaments, plate, bells and other gudds belonging to ye parish Church of Garstang,[12] taken in the towne of Preston before Sir Ryc[d] Houghton Knight, George Browne and Thomas Barton by thauctoryte of the Kyngs Commyssyon," on 18 November 1552.

"Imprimis ij chalyces, Itm iij belles in the steple one hande belle and ij sakring belles.   It' iiij vestyments wherof one is of grene satyn of brygges another of Redde satyn of brygges another of sylk w[t] bridds of

---

[10] *Notitia Cest.*, Chet. Soc., vol. xxii, p. 408.

[11] Canon Raines' *Lanc. MSS.*, vol. xiii, p. 229.

[12] The original *MS.* is much defaced, all the signatures are gone except that of Ryc. Houghton, and of "Garstang" only "ng" is left, but there is no doubt but that it refers to the parish.

M

gold, and one other vestment of redde tawny chamlette wt eigles of vellvet . . . . every vesyment.

In 29 Henry VIII. (1537–38) Robert the abbot of Cockersand granted the next presentation to the vicarage of Garstang to Sir William Powlet, knt., and John . . . . . . [13], but the abbey being finally dissolved in 1540, the right was probably never exercised, and in 1545 the patron was John Kytchen of Pilling, who in that year presented a vicar (see chapter v).

The advowson shortly afterwards passed to Christopher Anderton of Lostock, Esq. (son of Laurence Anderton, a descendant of the Andertons of Anderton), who presented a vicar in 1559, and by indenture dated 10 August 1569, granted a lease of the vicarage for twenty-one years to Thomas Anderton of Chorley, who was to pay 20l. per annum to Hugh Anderton the vicar.[14]

Christopher Anderton died 35 Elizabeth (1592–3), and shortly afterwards the advowson either reverted to the crown or was sold by James Anderton (the son of Christopher), as by deed dated 17 February, 4 James (1607), Gyles Simpson of London, goldsmith, and Sir Thomas Peyton of Knowlton, Kent, knt., in consideration of 900l., enfeoffed and confirmed to James Bushell of Evesham, Westmoreland, gentleman, and Bryan Wharnlye of Borwick, Lancashire, yeoman, all "that Rectory and Church of Garstange, all the Glebe Lands tythes &c. and all *manner of advowson* &c. for ever, to be holden of the King's Manor of East Greenwich in free and common soccage and not in capite nor by Knight's service." [15]

In 1620 the vicar was presented by the master of the Wards, and in 1650 the *Parliamentary Survey* shows that the patronage was then held by Christopher Anderton, who is described as a "Papist Delinquent." He is believed to have died that same

---

[13] Canon Raines's *Lanc. MSS.*, vol. xxii, p. 22.

[14] *MSS.* in possession of Richard Pedder of Finsthwaite house, near Ulverston, Esq.

[15] *Close Roll.*

year,[16] and the advowson passed to his eldest son, ffrancis
Anderton, who by indenture dated 16 September 1674, granted
the next presentment to John Anderton of Wigan, gentleman,
who in the year following conveyed it to Silvester Richmond, who
in 1679 (19 May) purchased the advowson from Sir Charles
Anderton of Lostock hall, bart. (eldest son of Sir ffrancis Anderton).[17]   For the next century the Richmonds were so intimately
connected with the parish that no apology is needed for here
introducing a notice of the family.

Henry Richmond of Ashton Keynes, Wiltshire,[18] was four
times married, and had twenty-five children ; the eldest son by
the third marriage (with Bridget Taylor) was Silvester Richmond,
who settled in Liverpool in 1662, where he practised as a phy-
sician, and for which town he was elected mayor in 1672.

In the troubled times of "the Lancashire Plot," Silvester
Richmond, who was then a justice of the peace, and Oliver Lyme
the deputy mayor of Liverpool, came under the unfavourable
notice of James II., who, having received information of what
was vaguely called "their misbehaviour," ordered their removal
from the offices they held ; after the Revolution they were both
re-instated.[19]

He married Sarah, a daughter of Clayton Tarlton of Aigburth,

---

[16] Christopher Anderton, who died 35 Elizabeth, was succeeded by his son James,
who died s. p.; and his estates passed to his brother Christopher of Lostock, whose
son Christopher is here named as the rector.

[17] *MSS.* in possession of Richard Pedder of Preston, Esq.   Francis Anderton was
created a baronet 8 October 1677.

[18] Family tradition makes this Henry to have been called Oliffe, and to have had
thirty-four children ; but his grandson, Oliffe Richard of Ashton Keynes, in a letter to
his cousin, Silvester Richmond, rector of Walton, dated 29 March 1736, gives the particulars as above quoted.   There were several Oliffe Richmonds of Ashton Keynes,
where the family had been settled for several generations.   Of Henry Richmond's
twenty-five children, only twelve lived to maturity, viz : first marriage, John and
Henry ; second marriage, Peter ; third marriage, Silvester, Oliffe, James and Francis;
fourth marriage, Jane, Edward, Mary, Elizabeth and Thomasin.

[19] Abbott's *Journal*, Chet. Soc., vol. lxi, p. 13.

Esq.,[20] who survived him, and by her Will left 50*l.* to the use of the almshouses which had been erected by her husband in Dale Street, Liverpool.[21]   Silvester Richmond died in 1692; a tablet in St. Nicholas' Church, Liverpool, records :

"Here lieth the body of Silvester Richmond, Professor of Physick and chyrugery, who after nearly 30 years indefatigable care and successful Practice in this town and county at last exhausted that life which had been so carefully employ'd in the preservation of many others.   He died the 16th and was interred the 19th April 1692."

His Will was proved at Chester, 22 June 1692, in which he bequeathed to his wife 2,000*l.* and all his household goods and plate, together with his "coach calash and horses," and after providing for his children and kinsmen, he leaves "to the poor of Liverpool 100*l.*," to the "Free School of Walton 10*l.*"   The advowson of Garstang church he left to his executors upon trust, "who upon every vacancy thereof shall p'sent thereto my son Henry or such of my grandchildren or their issue as shall be un-preferred to some Ecclesiastical Living, in case of any vacancy not to present any stranger but to use all lawful meanes to see that some of my grandchildren or descendants may enjoy the same."

He had issue, (1) Richard Richmond (vicar of Garstang, see chapter v); (2) Margaret, baptized at Liverpool, 25 May 1663, married alderman Richard Houghton of Liverpool, and had issue; (3) Silvester (of whom hereafter); (4) Proctor, baptized at Liverpool, 11 June 1667; (5) Sarah, baptized at Liverpool, 14 April 1669; (6) Harold or Harrill, baptized at Liverpool, 4 February 1671; (7) Henry (vicar of Garstang, see chapter v); (8) Peter, baptized at Liverpool, 14 July 1675.[22]

---

[20] Another authority gives daughter of Banastre Tarlton.   The Tarltons were established as merchants in Liverpool in 1559.

[21] *Charity Com. Report*, these alms houses have long ago been pulled down and others erected on Martin Dale Hill in their stead.

[22] Issue Margaret who married Mr. Tarleton, and left issue ; Sarah died unmarried; Ann married Mr. Tyrer, an Architect of Liverpool, and had issue ; Richard twice married, first to — Clayton, Second to Mrs. Booth ; Frances married Alexander Entwistle, and a daughter who married — Shaw of York.

Silvester Richmond, the second son, was baptized at St. Nicholas' Church, Liverpool, 1 October 1665 ; he was for many years a merchant and lived in Water Street, Liverpool, but appears to have subsequently removed to Acton Grange, in the parish of Daresbury, Cheshire.   In the Court Roll of the honor of Halton for 10 December 1720, his name is recorded as "steward of the Court to Robert Earl of Oxford" (then trustee for Earl Rivers), he is described as " Gentleman."   Acton Grange was the property of Sir Richard Brooke, Bart., of Norton Priory, whose daughter Frances Elizabeth, Silvester Richmond married ;[23] she survived her husband many years, and died at the age of 92.

The following epitaph was engraved on a monument in Darésbury church or church yard,[24] where Silvester Richmond was buried, 31 January 1746 :

Juxtim

Reconduntur Cineres

Sylvestri Richmond

de Acton Grange, Armig.

Viri, quem, ob egregias virtutes & merita, suspicerent omnes, & admirarentur, dignissimi.

Sumo fuit in Amicos affectu, in Deum reverentia, in Egenos liberalitate, in universos Fide & Benevolentia, Qvas quidem Ille virtutes adeo non ostentabat, ut sui nonnunquam dispar videri, & integerrumos ipsius Mores ultro dissimulare voluit.

In audendis periculis pectore fuit animoso, nee minus in adversis perferendis pio & constanti : cujus rei argumento sit geminata illa Plaga, quam Natorum eximia Spe juvenum acerbissimus casus inflixit.

Ecclesiæ Anglicanæ Fidem unicè amplexus, cultus solenniores veneratus Clerum singulari studio & observantia prosecutus est.

Annos paulo plus LXXXI vixit, plùres consecuturus

<hr>

[23] He had previously married a Miss Hyde.

[24] No monument now in the church.

si amicorum vota valuissent; si corpus, quam libet
firmissimum illud, par animi vigori contigisset.
Nec vitæ adeo longæ pertæsus, nec longioris appetens ;
nec sibi gravis, nec alijs, Dei opt. Max. Clementiâ
Christi solius meritis conciliandâ fretus Animam
candissimam generosissimam efflavit
Die Januarij 29
MDCCXLVI.

Silvester Richmond of Acton Grange had issue, (1) Mary,
born 22 May and baptized at Liverpool,[25] 3 June 1700, died unmarried ; (2) Brooke, born 4 June, baptized at Liverpool, 19 June
1701. Was a Captain in the Navy, died at Sea, and left no issue.
He married Rebecca Poole ; (3) Legh (vicar of Garstang, see
chapter v); (4) George, born 19 February, baptized at Liverpool,
27 February 1704 ; (5) Silvester, born —October, baptized at
Liverpool, 1 November 1706, entered the Brasenose College,
Oxford, 21 March 1724, took his B.A. 17 October 1727.   He
died (s. p.) whilst at the University ; (6) Frances, who was married
at Daresbury on 3 June 1732 to John Atherton of Walton Hall,
near Liverpool, Esq., and died in 1788, having issue, Catherine,
who married her cousin, Dr. Henry Richmond (see chapter v),
and Elizabeth, who married Michael Nugent, Esq.; (7) Letitia,
born 2 June, baptized at Liverpool, 21 June 1709, and died
unmarried.

Silvester Richmond (of Acton Grange), by deed dated 20 June
1740, conveyed the advowson of Garstang to his nephew, Silvester
Richmond, rector of Walton (see chapter v), who in 1750 (2 July)
sold it to Richard Pedder of Preston, gentleman.

The first representative of this family who settled in Preston
was Thomas Pedder, who served as a "gentleman soldier" under
captain Lynley.   He was probably living in Preston in 1657, as
on 16th May in that year he married Elizabeth, the daughter of
Richard Fielden of "Freregate," in that town, and in the Guild

---

[25] All these at St. Nicholas' Church.

Roll of 1662 appears amongst the in-burgesses the name of "Thos. Pether."

He was thrice married; secondly, on 17 July 1662, to Alice Fielden, widow, of Preston, who was buried at Preston in November 1678, and left issue a son, Thomas Pedder, baptized 17 February 1666-7, who left issue; thirdly, on 29 September 1679, to Dorothy Postlethwaite, by whom he had one daughter, Elizabeth, baptized 11 April 1680.

By the first wife Thomas Pedder had issue, Joan, baptized 16 August 1658, and Richard Pedder of Preston, linnen webster, who was baptized 26 October 1659, and was buried at Preston 24 March 1725-6, having issue, (1) Elizabeth, baptized 1690-1; (2) Richard (of whom hereafter); (3) Jennet, baptized 1695; (4) Paul, baptized 28 January 1696-7, who was twice married and had issue; (5) Peter, baptized 1 February 1699-1700, was married and had issue; (6) Philip, baptized 30 April 1702, was married and had issue.

Richard, the eldest son of Thomas Pedder, was baptized 12 February 1692-3, was mayor of Preston 1748-9 and 1756-7, and died 20 December 1762; he married (20 January 1711-12) Jennet, the daughter of John Reed of Preston; she was buried 31 May 1773; they had eleven children, viz: (1) Richard, baptized 1712, married a daughter of Robert Ashburner of Preston, he died 1744, leaving no issue; (2) Ellen, died young; (3) Edward, born in 1717, mayor of Preston 1763-4, 1770-71 and 1776-77, he married Katherine, the daughter of John Clayton of Stockport, 15 March 1737, and was buried at Preston 13 May 1789, leaving issue; (4) Thomas, died young; (5) Jane, died young; (6) Thomas, born 1729, mayor of Preston 1779-80, died December 1781, s.p.; (7) Jane, died in infancy; (8) Grace, married John Derbyshire of Preston, gentleman; (9) James (vicar of Garstang, see chapter v); (10) Matthew, died in infancy.

The present patron of Garstang church is Richard Pedder, Esq., late of Preston and now of Finsthwaite house, near Ulverstone (see chapter v).

In February 1571,[26] the rectory of Garstang with the tithes of "corne, grayne and haye, wool, fflaxe, hempe and lambe, and all other tithes whatsoever as well great as small and of all oblacions, fruits, profitts," were leased for a term of years (which had not .expired in 1615) to Edward Turner, for a yearly rental. Before Trinity Term 1615, the lease was assigned to Robert Bindloss of Borwick, Esq., who in that year lodged a complaint in the Court of Exchequer to the effect that George Mitton the vicar of Garstang "nott resting himselffe satisfied w[th] the endowm[ts]" of the vicarage, which was of the value of at least 100l. a year, and "soe much as where w[th] all the vicars ever since the endow[mt] thereof have rested themselves satisfied hath ever since hee became to bee viccarr by reason of his habitation and dwellinge w[th]in the said parishe, wrongfully claymed extorted collected and gathered &c. a great parte of all and every the Easter dueties and paym[ts] att Easter commonlie called the Easter Reckonings or Easter booke of all and every y[e] parishioners that is to saie the oblations plowe pence howse money otherwise called smoake money or smoake pence, w[ch] several paym[ts] hee the said George Mitton hath obtained although he doth well knowe and soe hath beene often informed that yo[r] orator doth paie rent for the same to his Mag[tie]." The vicar was ordered to answer the charges, but his rejoinder has not been preserved.

In 1622 Sir Robert Bindloss, knight, again appears at the Exchequer Court as complainant against Alexander Standish, Esq., and Richard Greene, gentleman, the matter in dispute being the tithes of the parish of Garstang. Amongst the witnesses examined were Henry Mercer of Newhall in Barnacre, gentleman, aged 53; John Saul of Winmarleigh, yeoman, aged

---

[26] In Baines' *Hist. of Lanc.* (second edition) it is stated that on 12 February 1571, the rectory, &c. was granted to Jane Kitchen for twenty-one years, she to pay to the curate 40[s] a year. No authority is given for this, and it is clearly incorrect. The particulars given about are from the "Exchequer Bills and answers, James I.," No. 156 at the Record Office. Robert Bindloss at the expiration of Turner's lease must have purchased the fee.

55; Robert Kitchin of Scurton, yeoman, aged 73; William Travers of Nateby, Esq., aged 64; Richard Blagbourne of Scurton, gentleman, aged 48; Christopher Walker of Netherwyersdale, yeoman, aged 65; and Richard Atkinson of Netherwyersdale, yeoman, aged 71. From the evidence produced, tithe corn appears then to have been let at the following annual rents, viz:

Tithe Corn and Barn of Winmarleigh - - 45*l*.

      „   „   Scorton - - - 43*l*.

      „   „   Bilsborrow - - 40*l*.

      „   „   Catterall - - 32*l*.

      „   „   Pilling - - - 42*l*.

      „   „   Barnacre - - 40*l*.

      „   „   Cabus and Cleveley 32*l*.

Wedecar mill paid a tithe of 8*d*. per annum.

Kemp's tenement (which about thirty years before 1622 was held by one Christopher Kemp) was held as part of the demesne of Wedecar, and for which a tithe of three measures of meal per annum was paid.

The rent paid to the crown by Sir Robert Bindloss was 40*l*. a year.

At the time of the Parliamentary Survey of 1650, the Tithes of the whole parish (except Claughton) were impropriate, and Sir Robert Bindloss was still the lay rector; they were then worth 313*l*. per annum, with the small tithes of the annual value of 30*l*. and 12*d*., which was paid to him by Richard Shuttleworth for a water corn mill in Bilsborough, called "Powle Milne," being a rent due by prescription. The vicarage had belonging to it a house and three acres of glebe land in Garstang, worth 3*l*. per annum, also a parcel of land and one tenement called "Stouthouse," which was then let for 17*l*. a year (but was worth twenty marks per annum), and was "deteyned from y*e* minister by John Greenwood of Lanc*r* upon p'tence of a Lease for a tearme of yeares yet is beinge made by Doctor Wildbore a delinquent late minister to y*e* use of Jane Rootes his kinswoman (see chapter v), who is now wife of y*e* said John Greenwood, a yearlie rent of

N

eighteen shillings beinge onely reserved out of the same to the minister of Garstang."

The tithes of corn and grain and all the small tithes of Claugton belonged to the vicar, and were worth 45*l.* per annum, the whole of the "profitts of the Vicaridge" being worth 60*l.* a year. The "hamletts of Barniker, Wyersdale, Cabus, Winmerley and Natebie beinge neere adjacent (to Garstang) and consisting of many hundred families," requested that they might be "annexed to the Market Towne and bee made a Parish," and that a minister might be placed there.[27]

By Indenture, dated 12 July, 12 Charles II. (1660) Sir Robert Bindloss, Bart., and Dame Rebecca his wife, conveyed "all that the Rectory, parsonage and church of Garstange, and all tithes and spiritualities" to William Standish, son and heir of Edward Standish of Standish Hall, Esq., in consideration of a marriage about to be celebrated between the said William Standish and Cecilia, the daughter of Sir Robert Bindloss.[28]

By deed, dated 1 September 1674, William Standish and Cecilia his wife conveyed the tithe-barn and tithes of corn, grain, hay, &c., of Catterall and Bilsborrow to Thomas Winckley of Preston, gent., it being agreed that out of the premises conveyed 20*s.* a year shall be reserved "towards the King's rent out of the Rectory of Garstenge," and that Thomas Winckley shall not be charged towards the repairs of the chancel of the parish church of Garstang.[29]   The present lay rector is C. H. L. W. Standish of Standish, Esq.

There were two chantries in Garstang Church, one of which was dedicated to "our Ladie," and was founded in the south-east aisle by Margaret, the daughter and co-heiress of Sir Robert Laurence of Ashton Hall, and wife of Nicholas Rigmayden of Wedacre Hall, Esq. (see chapter vii), who, by deed dated 3rd October, 7 Henry VIII. (1515), devised certain lands (which she

[27] *Parl. Survey*, Record office (Robert Bindloss was created a baronet, 16 August 1641).

[28] Original deeds in possession of Richard Veevers, Esq., of Preston.

[29] *Ibid.*

held in her own right) in trust, to the intent that the rents arising therefrom should be paid to an altar priest, for his yearly stipend, to sing, read, and pray in the parish church of Garstang. The office of priest was held from 1542-3 to 1544-5 by Thomas Laurenson, who, in the latter year, brought an action against John Rigmayden, the grandson of the founder, for refusing to pay the annual stipend.[30] Margaret Rigmayden died 10th August 1516. The lands and tenements with which the chantry was endowed in 1548 were of the yearly value of cvi^s viii^d without reprises.

The other chantry (probably dedicated to St. James) was founded by Roger de Brockholes, who was living in 1479,[31] and whose *Inq. Post Mort.* was dated 15 Henry VII. (1499). Henry Haye was incumbent here for some years, and was buried at Garstang 17th March 1577-8 ; his yearly salary at the time of the suppression of the chantries was xl^s and his board.

The date of the erection of the present venerable-looking church is unknown, but a great portion of it is very old, and altogether it is a noble specimen of a well-preserved parish church. In 1746 an inundation of the River Wyre overflowed the church-yard, doing considerable damage to the church, which in consequence narrowly escaped being handed over to the "restorers." In 1811 the church was reroofed, and the walls raised at the joint expense of the parish and Thomas Strickland Standish, Esq., the lay rector. In 1868 it was again repaired, the roofs were opened, the galleries and pews cleared away, and the chancel walls restored to their ancient pattern.

The church now consists of a tower (containing a fine peal of bells),[32] a nave, north and south aisles, chancel, chancel aisles, south aisle, chapel and vestry.

---

[30] *Duchy Records* and *Lanc. Chantries*, Chet. Soc., vol. lx, p. 199.

[31] *Lanc. Inquis.*, Chet. Soc., vol. xcix, p. 105.

[32] The bells are modern. In 1828 the vestry "resolved that a new cast of six bells, the tenor bell to be 12½ cwt., and the remaining bells in due proportion, be immediately procured," in 1829 130*l.* was borrowed "on the credit of the parish " to pay for them, and 2*l.* 14*s.* was paid for "carriage of old bells to London."

The nave is lighted by clerestory windows, which replaced the
old gabled windows in 1811, and between it and the side aisles
are strong and massive pillars.   The east window is a five-light
one of noble proportion and design, above the central light are
two figures, intended to represent some or other of the saints, but
which has long since been forgotten, and they are known as
"Moses and Aaron," and about them is a tradition that if the
glass which composes them should be taken out or destroyed,
that it will miraculously re-appear.   The tracery in the west
windows of the aisles are worthy of note, as also the three light
window erected in 1867 by Ann Bell, in memory of her parents,
Thomas and Esther Bell, and her brothers and sister, Henry
Bell, M.A., Richard Bell and Mary Ann Bell.   A new east
window was placed in the church in 1877.

The chancel is lofty and broad, and on either side are six
stalls with grotesque carvings under the seats, over the choir
vestry screen appears the following inscription which was formerly
over the stalls, "Bona consuetudo exeuciat quod mala extrucit.
Minus semper dicit quam facias," and above the door is inscribed,
"Pax ingrediem tibus."

The lady chapel or chantry is separated from the aisle by two
arches, and its flat roof is divided into square panels; on the frieze
and oak beams of the roof is inscribed, "In templo gentes caveant
simul esse loquentes.   Demon scribit ibi cuncta locuta sibi, A.D.
MDXXII hoc opus . . . . . Sancta Maria ora pro nobis."   The
Piscina still remains.

In 1836 the vestry underwent some repairs, and over the ceiling
was discovered a small room, which had in former times been
used as the priest's chamber, and in it were some of the brasses
now on the church walls.

In the north chancel wall was formerly an opening of two feet
square (it is now made up at one end), which was in all probability
used for the confession of lepers ; it certainly was not as has been
suggested a "squint," as it has no slant but opens full to the
east.

On the ground floor of the tower were (not long ago) the following rules, painted on the plaster.

"[Whoever] a Bell doth overthrowe
[Shall pay] two groate before hee goe
[And he that] ring^d with his hatte on
[Shall pay] two groate and then be gone
[And he that] ring^d with spur on heele
. . . . . ? that penalty shall feele
[And he that] dare an oathe sweare
[For that shall pay] two quartes of beare
[These Rules are] ould they are not newe
[But then the old] clark must have his dewe
                              S. R. B. M. J. Ringers."

The pulpit bears the date of 1646.

Over the north western door of the church is a niche, which probably at one time contained a carved figure of the patron saint.

In the church are the following inscriptions :

In South Chancel Aisle.

On Tablet,

"Hic sepelitur corpus Elizabethæ Leybourne olim Georgii Preston de Holkar ar^i felice minimæ natû nuper Georgii Leybourne de Cunsicke ar^i conjugis postq^m fuerat, Primo Joanni Sayer de Worsell ar^i secundo Nathanieli West ar^o ex nobili prosapia Westorum titulo de la Warre insignitorum orto cui filiam postea Roberto Plumpton in Comitatû Eboracensi ar^o nuptam pepertt in matrimorium data obiit die 16 Aprilis a^o Dñi 1687 Ætat 63."

"Here lye the bodies of Thomas Waringe and Ellen his wife who lyved together 34 yeres and above and had issve William now of Grayes Inne : and Thomas Wareing of London mercer and Ellen Waringe their daughter who died when she was of thage of 2 yeres or thereabouts. Ye said Thomas Waringe the father died in Anno Domini 1598 and ye said Ellen his wife died in the yeare of our Lord God 1606 and lived in good credit in the world and so accordingly made their end whose good examples God graunt wee all may followe   Amen.

> " Si bene vixeris in hoc mundo
> Salvus eris in secundo
> Quia qualis vita finis ita."

Near to this, on the same wall, is another brass, inscribed :

" Hear lieth the body of Mr. John Wareing the son of the Rev. Thomas Wareing Vicar of Garstang who died 24th October 1716."

There are also two brasses referring to the Banastre family.

" Here lyeth interred the Bodie of Christopher Banastre late of Preston in Amoundernes Esquire, sometimes Vice-Chancellor of the Countie Palatine of Lancaster for the space of 27 years the King's Maties Attorney Generall and one of His Maties Jvstices of the Peace qvorvm and oyer and terminer within the said Countie Baron of the Excheqvre at Lancaster Steward of the Borrough of Preston and Recorder of the Corpo⁻ration of Lancaster who after he had lived 74 years departed this life at Catterall vpon Thvrsday the 14th Jvne Anno Christi 1649.   Svnt nisi præmissi qvos periise pvtas.   Hodie mihi, Cras tibi.   R. L."

"Here lyeth interred the body of Joane Banastre widow relict of Christopher Banastre Esqr who after shee had vertvovsly and piovsly lived seaventy five years dyed at Catteral vpon Tvesday the twenty third of November Anno Domini 1669 and was bvried vpon Friday the twenty sixt of the same month.

" Esto fidelis vsqve ad mortem et Dabo tibi corontam vitæ."

On the north side of the altar is a marble monument bearing a full-length figure seated with a sword in the right hand. Inscribed is :

· " In Memory of Alexander Butler of Kirkland Hall and Beaumont Cote, Esq., who died the 6th May 1811, aged 79, descended from an ancient and honourable house ; he served his county in the important offices of high sheriff, constable of Lancaster Castle, deputy-lieutenant and magistrate, he chose an elegant retirement as most congenial with his literary and philosophical pursuits.   This monument was erected by his successor and heir, Thomas Butler Cole, Esq."

The following, on stone in the north aisle, all refer to members of this family :

"Elizabeth, daughter of Alexander and Elizabeth Butler, and wife of Mr. Singleton of Poulton, ob. 6 January 1737, æt 39.

"Elizabeth, wife of Alexander Butler, Esq., ob. September 19 1726, æt 63.

"Alexander Butler, Esq., ob. 23 July 1747, æt 74.

"Thomas Butler, Esq., ob. 12 November 1748, æt 53.

"Dorothy, wife of the above Thomas Butler, ob. September 13 1754, æt 47.

"Edmund Butler, son of Alexander and Elizabeth, ob. 27 September 1757, æt 58.

"Mrs. Langton, dr of Alexander and Elizabeth Butler, ob. November 14 1761, æt 59.

"Mrs. Crumbleholme, dr of Alexander and Elizabeth Butler, ob. October 25 1764, æt 46."

On the south chancel wall is a brass plate (which for many years was lying in the vestry) inscribed :

"Hoc tvmvlo inclvsus pastor pius integer Aynsworth.
Vitæ (dum vixit) fortiter ingenuus.
Pesticvs, ac Ivstvs cvnctus qvoque charvs amicis.
Pacifer et clemens dapsilis et sapiens.
Iste diem clavsit cvm sexagessimvs Annvs.
Et qvartus filivm consecvere suum.
        Obiit Februarii 16, 1609.
Expentans vocĕ dñi hanc veni.
In ipsivs meriti et mei amoris testimonium.
Ego G. F. R. C. posui." [33]

In North Aisle.

On marble slab (on the wall) :

"Near to this place lieth the remains of Eliz. Parker of Preston, relict of the late Rev. Willm Parker, who died 23rd April 1778.   Aged 63."

[33] The last three lines have been added at a later date.

"M. S.

"Here lieth y° Body of William Wakefield interred Decemb' y° 8ᵗʰ 1704.   Aged 51.

"Ætatem virtutem superans."

"In Memory of W. F. Lucas Esquire of Brock Side in the Parish of Goosnargh in the County of Lancaster, who died on the 24ᵗʰ Feb' 1828 Aged 54 years."

In the west end two brass plates record :

"Here lies the body of Michael Clegg, son of the Rev. Mʳ Clegg, now Schoolmaster of the Grammar School of Garstang, Minister of the Chapel of Ellel and Sherside, who departed this life 24ᵗʰ December 1729 and was buried the 26ᵗʰ of the same month.

"In pace quiescat in gloria resurgat."

"Here lies the Body of Sarah Varley, the wife of John Varley, who was born the 14ᵗʰ of February and died the 13ᵗʰ of March 1754. Aged 36."

On a stone :

"Here lyth the Body of Richard Blackburne Gent. who died September 21 Anno Domini 1724 ætatis 68."

In the north aisle of chancel, on a slab with raised letters :

"Here lye the remains of the Rev. D. Thomas Waring, Vicar of Garstang, who died October 20, A.D. 1722.

"Requiescat in pace."³⁴

A brass plate on a tombstone under the late Kirkland pew was inscribed :

"In Memory of Henry Abbot of Garstang who died the xxv day of March Anno Domini MDCLXXI in the xxv year of his age.

"Henry Abbot dead
This living song doth sing
O're hell I doe triumph
O I death where is thy sting."

³⁴ This was originally in the Sanctuary.

In the middle aisle is a stone bearing the following inscription :

"Iohannes Corles de Garstang Gen.

"Qui vitæ honestissime curriculum morti heu nimium præp opera,
Non matura tamen transiit obiit, Die Septembris septimo. Anno
ætatis suæ xxxv, Salutis vero nostræ MD.CCXXIX."

On the north wall are two marble tablets :

"In memory of
The Revd John Pedder, M.A.
41 Years Vicar of this Parish
Who died, May 6th 1835. Aged 67.
Also of Isabella, his wife,
Who died, October 5th 1798. Aged 30.
Also of Elizabeth, second wife and relic of the above.
John Pedder, who died at Ston Easton, in the County of Somerset,
June 5th in the Year of our Lord 1857. Aged 33, & was interred there.
Also of Ellen, an Infant, who died Dec. 28th 1815.
Edward, who died, October 24th 1835. Aged 29.
Maria, who died March 5th 1837,
(and was buried at Clifton,) aged 23.
Children of the said, Revd John Pedder,
and Elizabeth, his wife.
"Blessed are the dead that die in the Lord."

"Joseph, sixth son of
The late Revd John Pedder M.A.
Vicar of this Parish.
Died at Colombo, in the Island of Ceylon,
On the 26th day of July 1841.
In the 52nd year of his age.
In affectionate remembrance of
A beloved Brother, this monument is erected
By his surviving Brothers and Sisters."

In the church-yard the following monuments, &c., are note-
worthy :

At the north end of the church is a stone slab, upon which is a
full-length figure, which probably represents a priest, although,

from it being much mutilated and worn, it is impossible to pronounce with certainty ; the date and name have long since disappeared,[35] the hands are clasped, the folds of a garment, descending to the knee, are still discernable, as also a pointed hood-like head dress.   At the same end of the yard is another raised figure of a man, over which is a name and date now almost obliterated, but which Whitaker,[36] a century ago, deciphered as "Leonard Foster 1631."   A small square stone, which is reared against the chancel wall, bears an inscription which has been deciphered as "Elizabeth Foster 1632."   The registers, however, contain no record of the burial of persons of that name in 1631 or 1632.

On the southern side of the church, in 1855, was found, three feet below the ground, a heavy stone slab, on which is carved, in broad relief, a figure, probably of a knight, but the inscription is almost entirely gone.

On the northern side is a stone inscribed, "Here lieth the bodies of Mr. Joseph Waddesworth and Thomas Goose of Catterall, who died the 15th of February 1715" (see p. 73).

On the southern side of the church are the pedestal and broken shaft of an old cross.

There are, no doubt, many more old monuments in this church-yard which have had inscriptions upon them of local interest, but the stone used appears to have been of too soft a nature to withstand the weather, and consequently the letters and figures are, in some cases, completely effaced, and in others quite undecipherable.

[35] A woodcut of this is in Baines' *Lancashire* and Whitaker's *Richmondshire*.
[36] *History of Richmondshire.*

CHAPTER III.

ECCLESIASTICAL HISTORY CONTINUED.

GARSTANG CHAPEL.

(ST. THOMAS'S CHURCH.)

IN 1437 the Archdeacon of Richmond granted a license to the inhabitants of Garstang to have Divine Service performed in the chapel of Trinity, in that town, for one year;[1] probably this was rendered necessary in consequence of the non-residence of the vicar of Garstang (see p. 80), and the license may have lapsed at the end of the term.

In 1526 Adam Asteley was curate of Garstang,[2] and in 1562 "Dom. Thomas Parkinson" answered, with the vicar, at the visitation of the bishop;[3] it is possible that both these may have performed service at some chapel in the town of Garstang. A few years after the latter date a new chapel was built, or the old one repaired, as Robert Beck of Manchester, gentleman, by his Will dated 17th December 1566, gave "to the chappell of Garstang towards yᵉ bigging or making of challis there xviˢ viiiᵈ ;[4] the meaning of this bequest is, that the sum named was to go either to the building fund, or to be expended in the purchasing of a chalice. The parliamentary survey of 1650 sets forth that there was then a chapel in the town, but that it had no minister, yet an order of both houses of parliament, dated 17th June 1646,

---

[1] Reg. Bowett f. 70 (see *Notitia Cestriensis*, vol. ii, pt. ii, p. 412).
[2] *Inq. Post Mort.* of Will. Traverse.
[3] Canon Raines' *Lanc. MSS.*, vol. xxii, p. 276.
[4] *Ibid.*, vol. xiii, p. 282.

had been made to the effect that 50*l.* per annum, "out of the proffitts of the tithes of the Impropriate Rectory of Goosnargh," which was sequestrated, was to be devoted to the maintenance of a "Minister at the chappell of the Market Towne of Garstange," and a similar amount out of the impropriate tithes of Kirkham was to be used for the same purpose.[5]

In the west end of the chapel, which replaced the one just referred to, was a stone, upon which was inscribed, "This Chapel was builded by Richard Longworth, Esquire, Bailiffe, 1666." Garstang was not incorporated until 1680, and under the royal charter Richard Longworth was not bailiff until 1692, but it appears that the office of bailiff was recognized by the inhabitants prior to their incorporation.

There was a small bell attached to the chapel, upon which was lettered, "William Ballon and Henry Abboutt Balives of Garstang 1668."[6] In 1769, the chapel being in a decaded condition, was abandoned, and shortly afterwards the present church was built ; from a letter addressed by the inhabitants to the bishop of Chester, dated 31st May 1776,[7] it appears that the chapel was then going to be built by subscriptions, and that the residents wished to have it consecrated (the old chapel never having been consecrated), they also desired to have the site changed, giving as their reason, that Sir Edward Walpole had promised to give the land, but his agent having died he refused to execute the deed of gift.[8] It was proposed to call the new chapel *All Saints*, and a request was made that the holy communion might be celebrated on "Sundays instead of Saturdays," which was then the practice, as the curate had to attend at the parish church on regular communion days, and the writer of the letter adds, that he supposes "there is no other place in the whole kingdom where

---

[5] Minutes of Plundered Ministers.

[6] *Bailiffs' Records.*

[7] *Bishops' Register*, Chester.

[8] An entry in the bailiff's books confirms this as follows, "the site of the old chapel was granted on lease by Sir Edw. Walpole to Mr. Joseph Clarke, attorney-at-law, for a term of sixty years, from May-day 1776, and on which site he built the house now (1830) standing."

the sacrament is administered on working days." In 1848 the chapel was extensively repaired, consecrated, and a burial ground added; in 1874 the chancel and organ were built, and the church reseated. A handsome east window has recently been placed in this church, under which is the following inscription: "To the Glory of God and in loving memory of Richard Robinson of Garstange. This window was given by his wife and daughter A.D. 1878"; at the same time Mr. A. A. Simpson of Elmhurst presented a reredos of polished pitch pine. The stone font bears the following inscription, painted in black letters, Thomas Parkinson Hujus Curatus Hoc Deo Dedicavit M.DCC.XXXXXXX"; there is, however, no record of a curate of this name in 1770, and possibly the figures, in repainting, have been altered, and should represent 1723 (see page 102).

In the eighteenth century the Bailiff and Burgesses of Garstang appear to have taken upon themselves the management of the secular affairs of the chapel, and their records contain frequent allusions thereto, *inter alia,* the following:

1702 Rec^d Subscriptions towards repairing the chappell ...	02 05 00
„ Disb^d ffor Mosse for the chapell..........................	00 04 00
ffor a quar' and a halfe of slate and dressing it	00 01 03
ffetching it	00 10 00
To the Slaters for slateing and mossing the chappell and Towns Hall and their board wages	01 02 06
1716 Repaireing the chappell	02 02 06
„ p^d towards Pew and Matting (probably the Corporation Pew)	00 03 06
1725-6 Pd ffor Slate at the delfe for chappell.................	00 03 09
1730 „ Washing Surplus Cloaths	00 01 06
1732 Spent at severall times on the Clergy	00 13 02
1735 „ with Mr Chorley who gave Pray^r Book	00 02 00
1737 Rec^d Mr Sutton's gift towards a Bible	01 10 00
1739 Spent at Widd. Willowsey[9] the day her son preached at chappell...	00 02 00
1769 P^d for a Sacrament Certificate	00 01 00

[9] In 1733 a Robert Willacy was curate of Ribby-with-Wray; *query,* is this the one here referred to? (See *Hist. of Kirkham,* p. 63.)

THE CURATES OF GARSTANG CHAPEL.

NICHOLAS BRAY was the officiating minister here about the year 1626, when the parish registers record the baptism of Augustine son of "Nic. Bray prebit'." For some years previous to this he was the schoolmaster of Kirkland school (see chapter vi); he resigned in 1628.

JOHN WINCKLEY was curate of Garstang and possibly officiating minister here from 1637 to 164–, during which time he had two sons baptized. He signed the "Protestation" in 1641, and is described as "minister." He was the son of Edward Winckley of Preston, gentleman, and married Margaret, the daughter of Thomas Butler of Kirkland, Esq. (see chapter vii), and had issue, Thomas (baptized at Garstang 26th October 1638), who was the Registrar of the Duchy Chancery Office at Preston,[10] and William (baptized at Garstang 13th March 1639–40) a Fellow of Corpus Christi College, Oxford.

THOMAS SMITH, in 1648, signed the "Harmonious consent of the Ministers of the Province within the County Palatine of Lancaster," and styles himself "preacher at Garstang Chapel"; he was not here in 1650, as there was then no separate minister (see page 99).

"Mr EDWARD LAURENCE, Pastour at ye parochial chaypell of Garstang," was married at Blackburn before Randle Sharples, 25 March 1655–6, to Anne the daughter of William Marsden of Tockholes. This marriage is entered both in the Blackburn and Garstang *Registers* (see chapter iv).

THOMAS PARKINSON "was presented to the chapel" on 21 August 1723 by the vicar of Garstang, who guaranteed him 30*l*.

[10] Thomas Winckley married Frances, one of the daughters of James Hodkinson of Preston, and Elizabeth, his wife, widow of Henry Lemon of the same place, and had issue (see *The Reliquary*, vol. xvii, p. 173).

a year;[11] for some years previously he had officiated as curate of the parish church.   Thomas Parkinson was a collateral ancestor of the late Canon Parkinson, D.D., in whose delightful book, *The Old Church Clock*, some extracts are given from this curate of Garstang's *Diary*[12] (see chapter v).   He died young, but the exact date is not known.   In December 1729, a Mr. Huddleston was curate of the parish church, but we find no record of an appointment to St. Thomas' until 1735.

JOHN SUTTON was presented 5th January 1735-6;[13] he was a son of John Sutton of Newton-in-the-Fields, was educated at Winwick Grammar School, and took his B.A. at Trinity College, Cambridge, in 1733.[14] On leaving College he was appointed master of the Daresbury Grammar School.   He remained at Garstang at least two years (see p. 101), and was succeeded by

JOHN HUNTER, who, in 1737, was the schoolmaster of Kirkland (Churchtown) School.   In 1760 he was elected to the living of Broughton, near Preston, and was afterwards curate of Pilling (see *post*).

JAMES FISHER was licensed to the "curacy of the augmented chapel," 11 October 1762.[15] His duties were defined clearly — he was to assist the vicar on sacrament days, visit the sick, and teach a school — for which he was to receive eight guineas from the vicar, at least 5*l.* per annum from the parishioners, and the school fees.   He resigned the curacy on his appointment to the vicarage of the mother church (see chapter v).

JOHN MOSS was nominated, 24 May 1773, by James Fisher, then vicar of Garstang; he had previously been master of the

---

[11] *Bishops' Register*, Chester.
[12] The *Diary* is still in the possession of a member of the family.
[13] *Bishops' Register*, Chester.
[14] College books.
[15] *MSS.* in Church Chest, and *Bishops' Register*, Chester ; the latter gives date of appointment 9 November.

Brownedge School, near Cartmel;[16] he held the cure until his death, in 1799; he was buried at Garstang church on 17th September.

Mr. Hewitson, in *Our Country Churches*, describes this curate as "a very combative soul," and furnishes an anecdote respecting a dispute between him and the Duke of Hamilton's agent, which was "fought out at Wedacre Holmes."

WILLIAM WAYLES THORNTON was nominated on 17th January 1800.[17] He entered Emmanuel College, Cambridge, as a sizar 10th June 1799, and as a "ten year man" graduated B.D. in 1809.[18] In 1815 he was elected a burgess of Garstang, and in 1816 served the office of bailiff. He died in 1821.

JAMES PEDDER, licensed 8th February 1822, resigned on his appointment to the vicarage in 1835 (see chapter v).

THE REV. WILLIAM ARMITSTEAD, the present curate, was appointed in 1835.

PILLING CHAPEL.

Tradition says that a chapel was erected here in the time of King John, and there is some evidence to support this, for as Theobald Walter (see p. 39), between the years 1193 and 1199, granted the "Haye of Pylin" for the building of an abbey by the canons of the Premonstratensian Order, "there serving God," it is clear that a religious edifice of some kind was then in existence; Baines, in his *History of Lancashire*,[19] states that a chapel here is named in a charter of Robert Fitz Bernard to the hospital of St.

---

[16] *Bishops' Register*, Chester.

[17] His "Letters testimonial" were countersigned by the Bishop of Chichester (*Bishops' Register*, Chester).

[18] The college book affords no more particulars.

[19] Vol. ii, p. 537, second edition; he quotes no authority, and the charter is not named in the first edition.

John of Jerusalem, in the time of King John (see p. 23). The abbey at Pilling was never erected, but, subsequent to the foundation of Cockersand abbey, a grange was built where Pilling hall now stands, and doubtless attached it, or not far from, it was the small chapel dedicated to St. John the Baptist. In 1493 the Bishop of Lichfield granted a license to a devout nun, Agnes Bothe *alias* Schepard, who wished to leave Norton priory and live a life of solitude in a cell near the chapel of Pilling (apud capellam de Pylling in parochia de Garestang).[20]

In the rental of Cockersand (1501) appears the following entry, "M^d yat Annes Schepte hasse payn to James ye Abbott of Cockersand for her lyuing 11^s 11^d to me and vi^s viii^d to ye Cōvent."

In the map of Lancashire, dated 1598, preserved in the *Harl. MSS.* (Codex 6159), St. John's chapel is shown as then existing near to, but not attached to, the grange; in Mercator's map, a few years later, the chapel is marked but the grange is not; whilst the maps of Speed in 1610, Blome in 1617, and Janson in 1620, all show "Pilling hall" and "St. John's chapel" standing at some little distance apart. In 28 Henry VIII (1536–7) the land in Pilling, in the holding of the abbot of Cockersand, was worth 40*l.* per annum.[21]

After the final dissolution of Cockersand abbey in 1540, the chapel of Pilling shared the fate of the majority of the small Lancashire chapels, and fell into disuse and partial ruin. In the reign of Elizabeth divine service was again performed there, and an allowance of 10*l.* a year was made for the maintenance of the curate, who received "lodginge and dyett" from the farmer of the demesne lands. In the beginning of the next century, the necessary funds being withheld, an appeal, in 1621, was made to the king, the result being the following order:

An order vpon a Reference from ye Kinge touchinge ye Tithes of Pillyn in the county of Lancaster and findinge of a Curate there.

WHEREAS it pleased the Kinges most excellent Mat^{ie}, vpon a petition

---

[20] Chet. Soc., vol. lvii, p. 30.   [21] *Duchy Records*, xxv, c.c., No. 26.

preferred to his Highnes, with certaine articles annexed, by Thomas Jones
on the behalfe of himselfe and 60 other inhabitants of Pillyn, within the
Rectory of Garstange, in the countie of Lancaster, against Sr Robert
Bindlosse K^t, proprietor of the said Rectory of Garstange, for withdrawinge
the meanes and not mainteyninge a Curate att Pillyn chappell, within
the said parish, and for exactinge of Tythe of the inhabitants of Pillyn
wch they ought not to pay, with other informacons of vexation, extertion,
and oppressions therein conteined, to referr the consideracon thereof
vnto vs. Whereupon wee haue examined and fully heard the same
debated before vs deliberately, and doe thinke fitt that a competent
meanes be raised for the maintenaunce of a minister or curat of Pillyn,
wth the consent of the said Sr Robert Bindelosse and Richard Westmore,
gent., authorized for the peticoners by writinge vnder their handes as
agreed to be as followeth.

FIRST, that from henceforth there shalbee a minister from time to time
continually kept att the said chappell of Pillyn, to read and say diuine
seruice vpon all Sundays and vpon all holydayes appointed by the Church
of England, and to doe the other rites aud dutyes belonginge to the
diuine wor^{pp} and seruice of God vsed and allowed in the said chappell
in the late Queene Elizabeth her tyme

AND that towards the maintenance of the said m^{9}ster for the time
being, and the xl^s heretofore allowed out of or parcell of the xl^{li} rent paiable
to the Kinges mat^{ie}, his heires and successors, for the said Rectorie of
Garstange, shalbee yearly payd to the said m'ster att the audit att Lancaster as hath beene accustomed by his Maties receiver there; and
because the same funde of xl^s only will in no sorte mainteyne a minister,
the said Sr Robt Bindlosse, out of his charitable devocon and att our
instance and request, albeit itt seemeth vnto vs that hee is not therevnto
compellable by lawe, is contented and doth freely consent and graunt
for him and his heyres, to giue and pay yearly, foreuer, for the further
and better maintenance of the said m'ster for the tyme beinge, the yearly
fonde or payment of tenn poundes, to be paid halfe yearly, by euen
portions, out of the said Tithes of Pillyn, within the said Rectory of
Garstange, vizt, at Whitsuntide and Martymas.

AND the said Sr Robert Bindlosse is contented that if ye minister or
curate of Pillyn shalbee vnpaid his tenn pounds pencon, or any parte
thereof soe giuen him as aforesaid by the said Sr Robert Bindlosse forth
of the Tythes of Pillyn att the tymes aboue menconed, that then itt shall

and maybe lawfull to and for the said Curate and his successors to enter into and take to his owne vse all the tythes in Pillyn aforesaid, and the same to keepe and vse to his most profitt and comoditie vntill such tyme as the said Rent or payment and arrerages therof, if any such bee, shall bee fully paid and discharged to the said Curate of Pillyn for the tyme being. And whereas itt appeareth vnto vs that the ffarmer of the demesnes of Pillyn, who heretofore gaue lodginge and dye^{tt} to the m'ster there, as also that the rest of the Inhabitants within Pillyn who are to receiue spirituall comfort thereby, should likewise contribute to this soe pious a worke, wee doe therefore thinke fitt, wch is likewise consented vnto by the said Inhabitants by their agent authorized as aforesayd, that the Inhabitants for the time beinge, other then the said ffarmor, shall yearly pay for euer vnto and towardes the findinge of the said minister for the time beinge the yearly summe or payment of eight pounds halfe yearly, the same to be taxed and layd equally and reasonably by six or fowre of the most substantiallest men of the said Inhabitants, and for that itt is meete that the ffarmor of ye dem^{nes} there hauinge the best parte of the landes in Pillyn, and heretofore most charged with ye findinge of the minister, should contribute to soe goode a worke, ytt is therefore thought meete by vs that the said ffarmor, his Executors and Assignees, during his terme, and the Reverconers and their heires after the said Terme ended, doe paye yearly for euer vi^l xiij^s iiij^d towards the further maintenance of the said minister for the tyme beinge. AND wee thinke fitt that if the farmor of Pillyn, his executors or assignees, or the Reverconers or their heires after ye terme ended, or the Inhabitants for the tyme being, shall neglect their respecture payments to the said m'ster for the time beinge, or any time hereafter, contrary to the intent and true meaninge of this order and direccon. That in such case itt shalbee lawfull for the said Sr Robt Bindlosse and his heires to stay his and their said payment in their hands vntill the said persons soe makinge defaulte doe make and performe their paiments accordinge to the tenour and meaning of this order.

AND FOR the other parte of the peticon and schedule thervnto annexed, beinge for matter of Tythes, fforasmuch as the same doth concerne matter of right whether Tythes be due or nott and who ought to pay, and what tythes and in what manner, wch beinge matter of Title is fitt to be tried in the ordinarie course by lawe, wee thinke meete that if any the occupyers or Inhabitants, farmors or others, shall deteine his or their tithes of the landes aforesaid, Sᵣ Robᵗ Bindlosse or his heires shall bring his or their action against one or two of them at the most, that soe the rights and title of the same may by ordinary course of lawe come in question, and as the tryalls therin shall fall out, soe the rest of the Leasees and occupiers of Pillyn shall clayme the like ffreedome, to be bound or free, as the tryal shal happen with or against the said pˡᶠ or defᵗˢ in the said tryall, without further vexacon or suite on either parte wᶜʰ is likewise assented vnto by both parties AND for the tyth salte wee hold itt fytt the like tryall to be made and to be conclusive in the like manner to both partyes. AND if the said Tythes be evicted from the said Sᵣ Robᵗ Bindlosse or his heires, whereby hee or they haue no benefitt of Tythes to the value of tenne pounds out of Pillyn, but the same landes be freed of payment of tythes, wee think fitt that in such case the m'ster for the tyme beinge be maintayned by the owners of lands and inhabitants in Pillyn aforesaid, att their owne proper charge, by and with the like payment of twenty foure poundes viijˢ iiijᵈ ouer and besides the xlˢ issuinge out of the said Rent of the said Rectorie. And the tenne poundes payable by the said Sᵣ Robᵗ Bindlosse and his heires from such eviction of the tythes of Pillyn as aforesaid, vtterly to cease, in regard their Laydes in respect of their ffreedome of Tythes wilbee soe much the more of yearly value and worth vnto them. And for the rest of the articles vpon examination wee hold them nott fitt of any further proceedinge therein.

November 30 1621,

G. Cant. Geo. Coluert.[22]

Notwithstanding this order the parliamentary commissioners in 1650 report that, at "the chappell of Pillin" there is "noe minister but the Cure supplied by Mᵣ Lumley who hath beene silenc'd for severall misdemeanors, the Inhabitants being very many, humbly desire they may be made a Parish, and that a minister and competent maintenance bee alowed."

In 1675 a curate had been appointed, and from that time to the present the living has never been vacant for any lengthened period. Pilling, at the time, was a district almost isolated, the tidal waters of Morecambe Bay being kept off by the "dykes"

---

[22] Archbp. Abbot's Register, vol. iii, fol. 106, Lambeth Palace Library.

or cultivated embankments. The only access to the place (other than on foot) was by a track along the shore, over the marsh from Cockerham to Pilling Lane.

The only inn in the village was called "The Providence," it was situate in what was then called "The Higher End Lane," to distinguish it from Pilling Lane, which is now in Preesall parish, although the inhabitants of the extreme west of that district still pay tithes to Pilling. The road to Preesall and Stalmine was begun in 1780, whilst the road to Garstang was not made passable until 1808 ; previous to that date the farm produce was taken to Lancaster or Preston market. The Knot End Railway was opened in 1870.

Bishop Gastrell[23] gives the value of Pilling as 11l. 13s. 4d., of which 10l. was paid by the impropriator, and 1l. 13s. 4d. by the crown.

Sometime about the year 1716 the chapel was found to be too small for the increased number of inhabitants and a petition was sent to the bishop praying that a new one might be erected in the centre of the chapelry ; for the proper carrying out of this the bishop required certain securities, the nature of which will be seen from the following agreement : [24]

Whereas upon the humble petition of John Anyon Clerk, Robert Bennet, William Smith, William Hull and John Threlfall Minister and Chapelwardens of the Chapelry of Pilling in the County of Lancast[r] lately presented to the Right Reverend Father in God, Francis, Lord Bishop of Chester, on the behalf of themselves and the several Inhabitants freeholders and charterers of and within the said chapelry herein afterward that is to say Roger Hesketh of Northmeals in the sd County Esq., Robert Hesketh gent. son and heir apparent of the said Roger Hesketh, Edmund Hornby Esq[r], John Addison gent., William Bell, Richard Dicknison (sic) sen., Mary Thornton widow, Stephen Ribby, Thomas Bell sen[r], Agnes Bell widow, Ellen Kirkham, William Shepherd, Richard Tomlinson, Thomas Bell jun., Richard Dicknison, jun., John Mount, John Fox, Thomas Jollys, John Hey, Thomas Escam, William

---

[23] *Not. Cest.*, Chet. Soc., vol. xxii, p. 413.   [24] A copy is in the church chest.

Mason, Margaret Porter, James Tomlinson sen., Anne Sheperd, Joseph
Gardner, Henry Lea, Jennet Threlfall widow, Thomas Townson, Mary
Danson, John Noare, Jane Bond widow, George Tompson, John Jackson, James Tomlinson jun., William Clark, Jennet Bibby widow, Richard
Jones, William Bibby, Abraham Smith, James Procter, Henry Smith,
Philip Tompson, Margaret Hey, Robert Smithson, Henry Piccop, Elizabeth Williamson, Richard Clark, Thomas Tayler, Elizabeth Burton and
William Williamson, shewing and setting forth that at the time of the
erecting and building of the present Chapel in Pilling aforesaid (which is
now very ancient) there were but seven houses besides the Mannor house
in the said Chapelry.   That the said Chapel was originally built in the
east part and confines of the Chapelry near to the Mannor house, for the
conveniency of the Lords and owners of the Mannor and lands whereof
the said Chapelry consists (as had been esteemed).   And that the said
Chapelry, being then increased to above one hundred and forty families,
and the inhabitants thereof become very numerous, the present Chapel
was not near sufficient to contain them, but that there was an absolute
necessity for the same to be enlarged, or a new one to be built in lieu
thereof, and that as well the Lords and owners thereof (save some few
who either lived out of the s^d Chapelry or were in such circumstances as
not to contribute either to the Church or poor) were desirous & had
agreed to have a new chapel built (without any charge or trouble to any
that did or should oppose so pious a work) in the middle or center of
the s^d Chapelry (where the landlords were willing to give a convenient
piece of ground for a chapel-yard), most of ye Inhabitants living on the
West side of the s^d chapel, & there being very few families on the East
part of the s^d chapelry, and the s^d petitioners & their s^d petition praying
that they might have his Lordships leave and order to erect a new chapel,
intended to be twenty two yards in length and seven yards in brea[d]th
between the walls, & that they might make use of the materials of or
belonging to the present old chapel for that purpose, and that the chapel
yard of the present old chapel might forever be appropriated and secured
to and for the use of the Minister for the time being of the intended new
chapel, and the s^d Lord Bishop having considered of the s^d peticõn and
the purport and intent thereof, was pleased to give or promise his license
or faculty for the building of a new Chapel and converting and making
use of the timber & materials of the old one for that purpose, according
to the tenor of the s^d petition, provided and so as his Lordship had

sufficient security given him for and concerning the making and perfecting of a new chapel for the purpose in the s^d petition mentioned. Now, know all men by these presents, that the s^d Roger Hesketh &c.* * [names repeated] do hereby, for securing the erection & building of the said new chapel for the better satisfaction of the said Lord Bishop, for themselves, their heirs, &c., convenant, promise, grant, & agree, &c., that they or some of them shall & will, before the end of fourteen months next ensueing the date hereof, without any charge or trouble to any person or persons that have or hath or shall or may be ag^st ye building of such new chapel (other than such sumes of money wch they shall voluntarily give), erect and build, or cause to be erected and built, in good, sufficient, decent, and workmanlike manner, a new chapel, to be of such length and breadth as before menčõned, in or near the middle or centre of the said chapelry, to be for ever after ye erecting and building thereof repaired and maintained at ye charge of all the Inhabitants, Freeholders and Charterers of and within ye s^d Chapelry, &c. * * And the s^d Roger Hesketh & Robt Hesketh do hereby, for themselves, their Heirs, &c. * * covenant & promise to & with the said Lord Bishop, his successors & Assigns, that as well ye said chapel yard of or belonging to ye present old chapel as the scite or ground whereon the said chapel now standeth, shall for ever hereafter be appropriated, goe & remain to and for the sole proper use, benefit & behoof of ye Minister for ye time being of ye said intended new Chapel &c. * * And ye said Edmund Hornby doth agree, for himself, his Heirs, &c. * * to & wth ye s^d Lord Bishop, that as well the old Chapell yard as ye scite whereon ye same chapel now stands, shall for ever be appropriated for the sole use of the Minister, &c. * * For the true performance whereof they, the said Roger Hesketh &c. * * [names repeated] do hereby bind y^mselves, their heirs, &c. * * to the s^d Lord Bishop in the sum of three hundred pounds, &c., &c. As witness their hands & seals, ye third day of Oct. in ye year of our Lord 1716."

In accordance with the terms of this agreement the new chapel was built, and was consecrated in 1721. Of the old building nothing remains; but a few grass-covered, time-worn grave stones[25] mark the spot where "the rude forefathers of the hamlet sleep."

[25] The inscriptions are nearly all gone, the grave yard being unenclosed, and in summer time undistinguishable from the surrounding meadow; one inscription reads, "Richard son of Christop^r Clark of this town was buried here Feby ye x^th 1720."

The church as it now stands is a plain unpretending building of
stone; at the west end is a double-arched belfry containing two
bells, and over the south-west door is engraved a sun dial, with
the inscription, "Thus eternity approaches. G. Holden 1766."
On the key stone is the date "1717." On a stone near the bot-
tom of the door is carved "17 W ½ E. 28." The font, which is of
beautiful design, is believed to be several centuries old, as it is
the one used in the old chapel. Inside the church on the north
wall is the following:

"A.D. 1757.

This C[hapel] augm^t and A.D. 1759 Lands purch^d with £400
    Whereof given by
Q^n Anne's Bounty £200
By Exor^s of Wm Stratford L.L.D.^{26} £100
By other Benef^{rs} £100."

A marble tablet on the same wall records:

"In memory of Robert Preston born at Pilling April 20th 1761 died
at his residence Fir Grove near Liverpool November 19th 1833. His
integrity was inflexible his benevolence unbounded and deeply will his
loss be deplored by thousands of the indigent whom he was ever ready
to relieve.

This Tablet was erected by Margaret Dawson his grateful dutiful and
affectionate daughter."

Another tablet on this wall:

"In Memory of Benjamin Sykes, of Mains, Singleton, who lived
equally esteemed and respected in the character of a husband, Father
and Friend.

Died 23 June 1856, In the 74th year of his age. This Tablet was
erected by his Widow and surviving children."

In the church yard are the following inscriptions:

On a brass plate on a tomb stone,

"Near this place lies the Body of Richard Whiteside who was born
on the 25th of Jany 1737 and died on the 7th of Novr 1801. He was a

---

^{26} Commissary of Archdeaconry of Richmond, buried at Lancaster September 1752.

native and constant Inhabitant of Pilling where he resided on his own
estate by the cultivation of which and other agricultural employments
he supported a large family.   He was truly an English Yeoman, one of
a body of men whose value cannot be placed too high and whose number it is to be lamented are decreasing.   In discharging the social and
domestic duties he was an affectionate husband, Father, relation and
friend.   And by a general conduct towards his neighbours showed a
gentle and christian temper of mind.   This stone is inscribed to his
memory by Geoffrey Hornby Rector of Winwick who knew him long
and well, sincerely respected him and who thus records his sense of the
loss of this worthy man to the township of Pilling." [27]

On a plain stone :

"To the Memory of the Rev. James Potter the Minister of Pilling
who died Sepr 30. 1825.   Aged 69 years."

Another gravestone is   ·

"Sacred to the Memory of Sarah wife of William Sandham who departed this life July 27th 1800 aged 70 years.   She was the mother of
12 children four of which she had at one birth and lived three weeks."

The floor of the church was, so late as 1868, covered with
rushes.   The registers go back to 1621.   The parsonage house
was built in 1829; the churchyard was enlarged and enclosed in
1862.

The Curates of Pilling.

—— Lumley, though not the curate, appears to have officiated
at Pilling for some little time before 1650 (see page 108).

Oswald Croskell, "curat de Pilling, and Susannah Tomlinson was marryed ye 17th day of January anno 1675," so reads the
Register.   How long he held the office is unknown, but he had
probably a son who was living in 1725, to whom the Rev. Peter
Walkden refers in his *Diary*:

"Jan. 8th (1725) I came by the Old Hollins and over Wyre through
Scorton to Brother Miller's direct.   Jan. 9th Brother Miller having told

---

[27] Other inscriptions follow on the same stone.

Q

me in Garstang how Oswald Crossgill wanted pay for the goods bought at his sale some time since I determined to pay him and remove the goods . . . . . . I got John Macnoe and a horse and cart to follow me to Oswald's and paid him all I owed."[28]

RICHARD HARDY was curate in 1686. The *Register* for that year contains the following :

"Nov. 28.   James Bibby and Margaret Bibby[29] marryed at Pilling Chapel by me Rd Hardy, Curate."

On 15th November 1688 he was presented to the rectory of North Meols, where he died in 1708.[30]   He was the second son of William Hardy of Louth in Lincolnshire, merchant, matriculated from Pembroke College, Cambridge, 31st May 1667 (aged sixteen), and there graduated B.A. 1671, and M.A. 1674.

GABRIEL DAWSON, priest, was licensed to the curacy 28th January 1687–8 ;[31] he was probably one of the sons of Richard Dawson and Bridget, his wife, who, by his Will (proved 14th January 1665), left his house to his fourth son, Richard ; some land, near his house, to his eldest son, William ; and to "the rest of his children, 10*l.* a piece."

Gabriel Dawson was buried at Pilling 15th November 1692,[32] and letters of administration were granted to his son, Benjamin Dawson of Old Hulton, near Kendal, and Cecelia Johnson of Pilling.

That the Dawsons of Pilling were of the same stock as the Dawsons of Kendal there can be no doubt, and of this family was Robert Dawson, bishop of Clonfert in Ireland, who was buried at Kendal 3rd April 1645.[33]   Jacob Dawson of Highgate,

---

[28] Extract from Peter Walkden's *Diary*, Preston, 1866, f. 6.

[29] The Wills of James and Margaret Bibby were proved at Richmond 1705 and 1709.

[30] His successor was presented 24th July 1708.   He was not buried at North Meols. A Richard Hardy was vicar of Dean, near Bolton, 1636–45.

[31] *Diary* of Bishop Cartwright (Camden Soc., vol. xxii, p. 29).

[32] The entry in the *Register* looks like " *Wm.* Dawson Minister "—but no doubt it is intended to be *Mr.* Dawson.

[33] Monument in Kendal church.

Kendal, gentleman, had, by Mary, his second wife, a son Gabriel, who took his B.A. degree at Oxford in 1731 ; and a Gabriel Dawson of Farcross Bank was buried at Kendal 24th September 1701.[34]

THOMAS HUNTER was here in 1701, when a record of his marriage, on 11th January, to Margaret York of Lancaster is entered in the *Registers* ; nothing more is known of him ; he was probably of the same family as the two vicars of Garstang of the same name.

JOHN ANYON was nominated to the curacy 24th May 1715, by Roger Hesketh and Edmund Hornby, two out of the three lords of the manor (*i.e.*, they held with another the entire lordship) ; the other was reputed a Popish recusant.[35] The registers record the baptism of two daughters of this curate, viz : Jane in 1716, and Ann in 1718.

He was one of the petitioners for the building of the new chapel in 1716, and he held the living until 1731. In 1762 he was curate of Ribby with Wrea, in the parish of Kirkham,[36] and in 1769 he was also curate of Lund in the same parish, in which capacity he signed the "Recantation" of William Gant, Roman Catholic priest of Mowbreck, which was read in Kirkham church 28 May 1769.[37] He died in 1770, aged 86.

JOHN COULTON was nominated 10 September 1731,[38] and was here until 1758.

GEORGE HOLDEN was born in 1720, and was probably a native of Yorkshire, in which county he held an estate called

---

[34] Registers kindly furnished by G. E. Moser, Esq.
[35] *Bishops' Register*, Chester.
[36] *Hist. of Kirkham*, p. 64.
[37] This tract was published in Manchester in 1769 ; it is now very scarce.
[38] *Bishops' Register*, Chester.

Birch Hill, in Easington Dale Head, in the parish of Slaidburn.[39] Sometime before 1753 he was appointed to the office of second master of the Free Grammar School of Bentham, near Lancaster, and in that year, on 20th September, he was there married to Jane, the daughter of Marmaduke and Alice Brooks.[40] On 11th May 1758 he was nominated to the curacy of Pilling,[41] which he held until September 1767, when he was preferred to the perpetual curacy of the little chapel at Tatham Fell, in the parish .of Tatham, where he lived at a place called "the Green," which, at that time, belonged to the chapel.

George Holden was a great mathematician and a good scholar, and was the author of an annual publication entitled *Holden's Tide Tables*, for the compilation of which he is said to have received a government grant. Local tradition says that he was a little hump-backed man, with one arm shorter than the other. Several characteristic anecdotes are told of him, as, for instance, that one Sunday having nearly completed his three miles[42] walk from his house to his chapel, he suddenly discovered that, in one of his tide calculations, he had left out a cipher; back he at once turned and corrected his tables, but, adds the octogenarian narrator, "there was no preaching at Tatham Fell that day." Holden was also somewhat of a religious controversialist, and on one occasion he was called into the "Punch Bowl Inn" to argue with the Roman Catholic priest, who, getting the worst of the discussion, lost his temper, and on Holden's saying that "God made man upright at first," he thundered out in reply, "then who the devil made the hump-backed ones"?

George Holden died in May 1793, and was buried at Bentham,

[39] The *Parish Registers* record a baptism of Maria Holden of Dalehead in 1727, but not that of George Holden.

[40] Marmaduke Brooks lived in Higher Bentham and was a man of good position; his daughter Jane was baptized 26th June 1731.

[41] *Bishops' Register*, Chester.

[42] "The Green" was nearly three miles from Tatham Fell, and about a mile from Bentham church.

where a monument was erected to his memory, and which bears
the following inscription : [43]

"S. M.

Reverendi et apprime docti.

Georgii Holden

Qui Anno 1793 Ætatis 70

Privato et publico Luctu merito deploratus

Vitâ decessit.

Necnon

Janæ Uxoris ejus,

Fœminæ tali conjuge dignæ

Anno 1781 Ætatis 50

Obiit."

His Will was proved at Lancaster 11th June 1793 ; the following is a brief abstract :

" I, George Holden of the Green, in the parish of Tatham, clerk, &c.,
devise to my son George Holden, all my estate called Birch Hill,
situate in Easington Dale Head, in Slaidburn, chargeable with a payment of 200*l.* to my daughter Catherine, wife of the Rev. Mr. Johnson
of Doncaster ; and 100*l.* to my daughter Jane, wife of Daniel Elletson
of London, Esq.; I give 20*l.* to my daughter Hannah, wife of Christopher
Procter of Skipton ; to Alice Holden, all my estate in Upper Bentham,
consisting of five dwelling-houses and a barn, with two crofts and gardens ;
to my son George, my three book cases with all my Latin and Greek
books, my mathematical books, either printed or in manuscript, my
Hadley's Quadrant sector and scales, and all the books and instruments
useful in navigation, and also all my books, papers, and instruments used
in calculating the Liverpool Tide Table, upon condition that he will give
to my daughter Alice all the profits of the Tide Tables for two years
after my decease ; to my grandson George Holden, my silver watch ;
to my grandson George Holden Procter of Skipton, 5*l.*, and the like sum
to each of the children of my daughter Jane Elletson ; to my daughter

---

[43] The monument consists of three black slabs, with stone divisions, with white
marble rim, &c. Bentham church has recently been rebuilt, but the rector (the Rev.
Edgar Sherlock), to whom I am indebted for many of the above particulars, has
assured me that the monument will be cared for and replaced.

Alice, my writing desk, silver pint, and my best feather bed; all my other books, in English and French, I give to my three daughters, with a desire that they will not sell them but divide them equally.

"I appoint George and Alice Holden executors of this my last Will."

He had issue: Francis, baptized at Bentham 19th June 1756, buried 29th November following; George (of whom hereafter); Hannah, baptized at Pilling 29th March 1760, married Christopher Procter of Skipton, and had issue; Elizabeth, baptized at Pilling 8th August 1762, died before 1793; Jane, baptized at Pilling 16th April 1765, married Daniel Elletson of London, Esq., and had issue; Catherine, baptized at Tatham Fell 20th October 1767, married the Rev. —— Johnson of Doncaster, and had issue; Alice, baptized at Tatham Fell 25th March 1770, unmarried in 1793.

George Holden was baptized at Bentham 29th December 1757. About the year 1781 he obtained the mastership of the Free Grammar School of Horton-in-Ribblesdale, where he was married, on 14th September 1782, to Ann Procter of that parish. On 21 May 1798 he was instituted vicar of Horton, of which church he owned the advowson. He succeeded his father to the perpetual curacy of Tatham Fell, which he held until his death, continuing, however, to live at Horton, where he died in December 1820; a marble tablet in the church bears the following inscription :

"In Memory of the Rev. George Holden, LL.D., for many years Head Master of the Free Grammar School of Horton-in-Ribblesdale, and minister of this church; he died 31st December 1820, aged 63 years. This monument was erected by some of his pupils as a tribute of grateful respect to his memory." [44]

Dr. Holden continued the Tide Tables begun by his father. He was a man of high classical and mathematical attainments.[45] He

---

[44] He and his wife were buried at the west end of the church-yard. Against the end of the church is a stone tablet, recording the death of the latter; she was buried 7 July 1794, aged 36. For some of the above facts I have to thank the Rev. Joseph Senior, LL. D., vicar of Horton-in-Ribblesdale.

[45] Like his father, he had one arm shorter than the other.

left issue, one son, George Holden, who, in 1811, was instituted
to the vicarage of Maghull near Liverpool, where he died, and
was buried 19th March 1865, aged 82 years.   He was never
married.   He was a good classical scholar, and was the author
of several theological works.[46]

CUTHBERT HARRISON was nominated, on the resignation of
the last curate, 15th September 1767.[47]   He was the second son
of Richard Harrison of Bankfield in Singleton, in the parish of
Kirkham, gentleman, and Agnes, his wife, who was daughter and
heiress of the Rev. —— Crombleholme, vicar of St. Michael's-le-
Wyre.   His great grandfather was the Cuthbert Harrison who
was for some years curate of Singleton.[48]   Cuthbert Harrison
of Pilling was a student at Trinity College, Cambridge, where he
took his B.A. in 1766 ; he died at Clifton, in the parish of Kirkham, 1st June 1790, and was buried at Singleton, aged 46.   He
was never married.

JOHN HUNTER was nominated to the curacy 1st October 1774;
he had been appointed master of Kirkland (Churchtown) school
in 1737, and a little later to the curacy of St. Thomas' church,
Garstang, which he resigned in 1760 on his preferment to the
living of Broughton, near Preston, which he held until his appointment to Pilling, where he died in the year 1781.

WILLIAM BATESON was appointed, 15th October 1781,[49] on
the death of John Hunter ; he resigned in 1798.

THOMAS GODFREY was nominated 17th October 1798.[50]   He

[46] Inter alia, "Scripture Testimony to the Divinity of our Lord," "Proverbs of
Solomon," "Holden's Ecclesiates," "The Christian Sabbath," and "Dissertation on
the fall of man."   He was appointed vicar of Horton in 1821, but resigned it in 1825.

[47] Bishops' Register, Chester.

[48] See History of Kirkham, Chet. Soc., vol. xcii, pp. 50, 189.

[49] Bishops' Register, Chester.

[50] Ibid. (A T. Godfrey was living at Pilling in 1792 ; his name then occurs in the
Registers).

had been assistant curate from 1795 to that date. He resigned in 1802, and was instituted to the vicarage of Melton Mowbray in 1820, which he held until his death in 1832.

At this time Peter Godfrey of East-Bergholt, county Suffolk, Esq., was patron of the living of Melton Mowbray.

JAMES POTTER was nominated 8 December 1802;[51] he was the son of James Potter of Ellergill, in the parish of Orton in Westmoreland, and Elizabeth his wife; he was christened at Orton church 5 September 1756.

Before coming to Pilling, James Potter held curacies in the neighbourhood of Whitehaven and at Woodplumpton. He was an honest, straightforward, yet, withal, free-and-easy sort of man, who specially commended himself to the "hearty lads of Pilling," as they were called half a century ago. Many tales are told about him, most of which have doubtless been exaggerated and contorted; that he could preach well, and, if need be, fight well, however, may be accepted as true,[52] as also that he was respected by all his parishioners. He died 30 September 1825, aged 69, and was buried at Pilling (see page 113).

JAMES DAWSON BANISTER succeeded the last curate. He was appointed in 1825, and resigned in 1876.

JOHN WILSON WAITHMAN, M.A., is the present vicar.

CALDER VALE CHURCH,

Dedicated to St. John the Evangelist, was consecrated 12 August 1863. The cost of erection was 2,500l., which was raised by subscription; it contains a handsome Caen stone pulpit, erected to the memory of W. J. Garnett of Quernmore Park, Esq.

During the building of the church the Rev. Thomas Carter (afterwards vicar of Littleborough) was the curate-in-charge.

---

[51] *Bishops' Register*, Chester.   [52] See Hewitson's *Our Country Churches*.

From 1863 to 1868 the incumbent was the Rev. Edward Wright, who was succeeded by the present vicar, the Rev. John Gornall. Calder Vale is now a distinct ecclesiastical parish, and contains a population of 836.

WINMARLEIGH CHURCH,

Dedicated to St. Luke, was consecrated in 1876. The incumbent is the Rev. T. B. Armitstead, B.A., chaplain to Lord Winmarleigh.

BONDS ROMAN CATHOLIC CHURCH.

In 1784 the Catholics built a chapel in Garstang, which was abandoned when the handsome Gothic church in Bonds was erected in 1858. In 1825[53] the Rev. Michael Hickey, a native of Kilkenny, was appointed priest in Garstang, and it was mainly through his instrumentality the church, presbytery, and schools in Bonds were, at a cost of 7,000l., erected. Father Hickey died 12 August 1871,[54] and was succeeded by the Rev. Canon Seed, who died at the residence of his brother, Mr. Henry Seed of Stirzaker house, Catterall, 8 March 1877. He was the son of James Seed of Heaton hall, and was educated at Ushaw college.

CLAUGHTON ROMAN CATHOLIC CHAPEL.

We have discovered no evidence of an earlier chapel here than the one now in existence, which was built in 1792. The list of priests who have been stationed at Claughton, however, goes back to the middle of the seventeenth century, and service is said to have been performed prior to the erection of the chapel in the priest's house, which was built in 1682[55], and there was a private chapel at Claughton Hall at a very early period (see p. 79).

[53] John Barrow, a nephew of Rev. John Barrow of Claughton, was priest here from 1790 to 1811.
[54] For a description of this church see Hewitson's *Our Country Churches*, p. 490.
[55] Stone over the door bears initials "R. T." (Richard Taylor), and "1682."

R

The following is a list of the priests who have served this mission,[56] viz.:

EDWARD WALMSLEY prior to 1672.

EDWARD BLACKBURN was appointed in 1672, and was buried at Garstang, 26 September 1708–9.

RICHARD TAYLOR, nephew to Edward Blackburn; he built the priests' house in 1682.

ROGER BROCKHOLES, son of John Brockholes of Claughton (see chapter vii).

R. BIRTWISTLE

JAMES PARKINSON COTTAM died in 1766.

JOHN BARROW, a native of Westby, in the parish of Kirkham, was priest here for forty-five years; in his youth he served for seven years on board a man-of-war. He died at Claughton in 1811, aged 76 years.

ROBERT GRADWELL was born at Clifton, in the parish of Kirkham, 26 January 1777. He was one of the professors of Ushaw college from 1802 to 1809; he remained at Claughton until 1817, when he was appointed rector of the English college at Rome; in 1828 he was appointed as coadjutor of the London district, at the same time being consecrated bishop, with the title of bishop of Lydda. He died in London 15 March 1833. He was the author of *Dissertation on the Fable of Papal Antichrist,* 1816, and other treatises.

HENRY GRADWELL (brother to Robert Gradwell) was also

born at Clifton; he officiated here for forty-three years. The erection of the schools in 1853, and the formation of the present sanctuary, were due to his exertions; he died in May 1860, aged 67, and was succeeded by his nephew,

ROBERT GRADWELL, who had assisted him for some years before his death, and who is now in charge of the mission.

SCORTON CATHOLIC CHAPEL.

The present chapel was erected in 1861, and replaced a small thatched building, which in its early days was used as a clogger's shop on week days.

The following is a list of the priests appointed to Scorton : [57]

Christopher Jenkinson before 1745.

John Sergeant 1745 to 1795, in which year he died.

James Lawrenson 1796 to 1826.

John Dixon 1826 to 1830.

John Woodcock 1830 to 1837.

Thomas Gillett 1837 to 1838.

Robert Turpin 1838 to 1863.

Dr. Ilsley[58] 1863 to 1868.

Austine W. Splaine 1868, and now in charge.

GARSTANG INDEPENDENT CHAPEL.

The date of the building of this chapel is unknown, but it is probably about a century old. In 1725 David McMurry was the Independent minister at Garstang.[59]

GARSTANG WESLEYAN CHAPEL

Was built in 1814. John Wesley was twice at Garstang, in 1765,

[57] Hewitson's *Our Country Churches.*
[58] President of the English College at Lisbon.
[59] Extracts from the *Diary* of the Rev. Peter Walkden, p. 24.

when he was the guest of James Edmondson,[60] and in 1770, when he preached in the Independent chapel.[61]

SCORTON WESLEYAN CHAPEL.

The site of this chapel was given by the Duke of Hamilton and the expense of its building was defrayed by George Fishwick of Spring Field, Scorton, Esq.;[62] it was opened in September 1842.

NATEBY BAPTIST CHAPEL,

Or, as it is sometimes called, "Nook Chapel," was opened in 1839. There is a graveyard adjoining it.

PILLING WESLYAN CHAPEL

Was erected in 1813.

BILSBORROW WESLEYAN CHAPEL

Was built in 1815.

BONDS FRIENDS MEETING HOUSE

Was built in 1828, mainly through the instrumentality of the late Richard Jackson[63] of Calder Vale and his brothers.

---

[60] Jas. Edmondson was buried near the pulpit in the Independent chapel.

[61] R. Allen's *Methodism in Preston.*

[62] George Fishwick was the fourth son of Webster Fishwick of Burnley, and was born 5th June 1789, and died 19th October 1854. (See *History of Goosnargh* and *Wesleyan Mag.* 1855).

[63] Richard, John and Jonathan Jackson came to Calder Vale from Spout House in Wyersdale, where the family had for some time been settled.

CHAPTER IV.

THE CHURCHWARDENS AND THE PARISH REGISTERS.

GARSTANG had, no doubt, at one time, its regular constituted body of "sworn men," like Lancaster, Preston,
Goosnargh, and Kirkham,[1] but the distinct features which mark
the select vestry in these places have not been preserved here.

The oldest vestry book only dates back to 1734, and from it
we glean the following items, which show that the parish work
was entrusted to four churchwardens and twenty-four sidesmen,
and that the parish itself (Pilling not being included) was divided
into four quarters, each of which returned one churchwarden and
six sidesmen, the latter being always called "the gentlemen
sidesmen," and apparently elected for life, or during the good
will of the parishioners.

A List of the names of the Gentlemen Sidesmen for the
Parish of Garstang in the year of our Lord one thousand seven
hundred and thirty four :

FOR GARSTANG QUARTER.

Alexander Butler, Esq. (erased and over it Mr. James Raby.)
Mr. William Sturzaker (William erased and Jas. inserted).
Mr. Charles Sallom.
Mr. John Wakefield.
Mr. —— ——

---

[1] See *History of Kirkham*, p. 88, and *History of Goosnargh*, p. 51.

For Wiersdale Quarter.

Mr. Edmund Winder.

Mr. Jervise Burton (erased, over it Will. Hellme).

Mr. Richard Mason.

Mr. Brian Parker (erased, and Joh. Gardiner inserted).

Mr. John Cortes.

Mr. Edward Fox.

Barnaker Quarter.

Mr. Thomas Goose.

Mr. Thomas Graves.

Mr. John Dunderdale.

Mr. Thomas Dunderdale (erased, and Robert Blackburne inserted, which is also struck out, and James Carpenter substituted).

Mr. Richard Parkinson (erased, and Henry Walter inserted, and afterwards J. Bradley).

Mr. James Corles (erased, and Mr. Richard Cortas inserted).

Claughton Quarter.

Mr. Thomas Whitehead.

Mr. Richard Goose.

Mr. John Sherrington.

Mr. John Sallom.

Mr. John Weaver (erased, and Mr. Rowland Parkinson inserted).

Mr. Edward Harrison.

Other lists follow; the next is dated 1755, and, as in the preceding one, when a vacancy occurs the name was simply struck out and another inserted.

CHURCHWARDENS, 1734.

William Deane of Nateby, for Garstang Quarter. His assess^{mt} are 12l. 10s.; disburs^{mts} 12l. 10s.; all paid.

Richard Johnson of Bilsborough, for Mr. Benjamen Whitehead, for Claughton Quarter. His assess^{mts} are 14l.; disbur^{mts} 14l.; all paid.

John Cartmell of Cabus, for Wiersdale Quarter.

Henry Cottam of Barnacre, for Robert Shepherd of Bonds, for Barnaker Quarter.

1735.

Robert Borrah of Winmarley, for Garstang.

Will. Sudall of Catterall, for Claughton.

John Shaw, for John Story of Wiersdale, for Wiersdale.

Edwd Smith of Barnaker, for Barnaker.

This List is complete to 1777 ; the next two years are wanting ; in 1780 (and afterwards), the churchwardens are not named (as such), but the payments, &c., are recorded thus :

GARSTANG QUARTER.

"Ri. Singleton of Winmarley collected by 12 Fifteens 25*l.*; disbursed 25*l.*

The vestry books contain nothing more of historical interest.

A scrap of paper (preserved in the church chest), probably a portion of one of the churchwardens' accounts, amongst other items, contains :

"13 April 1784 Robert Hornby's Bill. Whipping Dogs out of church 3*s.*"

"Easter 1791, for the same service 5*s.*, and for Rushing the church 3*s.*"

THE PARISH REGISTERS.

The oldest volume commences in 1567, and is in a fair condition ; the registers are, from that to the present, complete, with the following exceptions, viz., January to June 1601, January to March 1609, September to December 1653, April 1659 to December 1660, which are wanting.

The title of the first volume is as follows :

The Boke of Regester or declaration of a^l chris⁵ Weddings and Burialls minēstred and donne in the Parish Church of Garstange sence the — November in the ix yeare of the regne of our Sov⁹ringe lady Elizabeth by the grace of God Queene of England france and ireland. Anno Dñi 1567.

And in this bocke a *C.* standeth for Christening *M.* for Wedinge and *B.* for Buriall.

1567.
November.

C. B. John Ortoun, the sonn of James Orton, was baptised and buried the ij day.[2]

C. Anne Wilkinson, doughter of Robert Wilkinson, the iv day.

C. John Cartmell, son of Thomas Cartmell, the xix day.

C. John, the sonne of Christopher Brockbanke, the xiij day.

December.

C. Albanie Butler, sonn of Robert Butler, was baptised the xxiij day.

B. George Butler was buried the xxxj day.

Januarie.

C. Henrie, the sonn of Hugh Kyghley, the xiij day.

Febrewarie.

C. Ellen Taylier, doughter of John Taylier and Ellen simpkinson, the vi day.

C. Wiłłm Cartmell, sonn of James Cartmell, the xxvi day.

March.

C. Rychard, sonn of Robert Huberstie, the iij day.

C. Katherine, the doughter of Rychard Whittingham, the same day (xv).[3]

1568. July.

C. James Butler, son of John Butler of Kirkland, Esq., the xv day.

---

[2] This is the first entry.   [3] Buried 11 April 1568.

Januarie (1568).

M.   Thomas Sikes and Elizabeth Tomlinson the xxviii day.

1567.   December.[4]

B.   Johanna ux' Nicolas Cartmell, the xxxi die.[5]

B.   George Butler eodem die.

1567.   Januarie.

C. B.   Johanna france, doghter of Robart france, was baptized and buried the xviij die.

March.

B.   Margaret Plesington the xviij die.

1568.   September.

B.   John Rygmayden de tungstall[6] the vi die.

februarie.

B.   Nicolas Walker de Garstange the xiij die.

1569.   May.

M.   Thomas Hodgkinson and Ana Hoghton xv die.

M.   Henri Bee and Grace Clarkson the same die (xii).

August 1569.

B.   John Stirzaker de Kyrkland the xiv die.

C.   Jane doughter of James Chippindall de Natebie the...

1570 Aprille.

C.   Thomas the son of Robert Butler de Kirkland the xxii die.

July.

C.   Henrie son of Mr. John Bould the xviij die.

B.   Anne wiffe of the said John Bould the xxx die.

John Bould was second sonne of Sir Richard Bolde of Bold in Lancashire, and this Anne his wyffe was daughter to Sir Thomas Langton Knight and Baronet of Newton in Lancashire.[7]

---

[4] The burials, baptisms, and marriages are arranged in "batches," as if transcribed from separate books.

[5] Before this the word is written in English.

[6] Tunstall-in-Lonsdale.

[7] This note appears to have been added to the Register.

S

September.

C. Robert, son of Antonio Calvart j die (Buried the 22 day).

November.

B. Anne, daughter of Thomas Whittingham the ij die.

B. John, son of Robert Charnocke, the xvj die.

1572. Jounarie.

C. Ann, doghter of Mr. Rychard Travis the viii die.

B. Elizabeth Rygmayden de Wedicar the xxj die.

Aprilli.

B. Ellen, the wife of Christopher Rygmayden the viij die.

M. francis fidler and Alice Singleton the xij die.

October.

M. John Rygmaden and Issabell Allerson, the ij die.

1573.

Januarie.

B. Wylliam, son of George Crocke, buried the xxviij die.

ffebrewarie.

M. Richard Billin and Elizabeth Crocke was married eod die (the 3rd).

March.

B. Christopher Rygmayden was buried the viij die.

B. A child of Mr. Tildesleys was buried the xviij die.

May.

M. Mr. Walter Rygmadĕ and Anne Tyldesley the xxi die.

1574

May.

C. Willm, son of Robert Butler, was baptized the xx die.

Auguste.

C. James, son of Rychard Bowers, was baptized the xi die.

C. John, son of Mr. Robert Braidill, the xxiij die (buried 3rd November).

November.

B. Wylliam Kyrebie was buried the x die.

C. William, son of Robert Plesington, was baptized the
    xviii die.

1575.

C. Edward, son of Mr. Richard Braidill, was baptized
    the xxvi die.

C. frances, doghter of Mr. Rychard Travis, was baptized
    the vij die.

1575–6. Januarie.

C. Grace, doghter of Mr. Robert Plesington, was baptized
    the viij die.

C. Jane, doghter of Mr. Walter Rygmayden, was bap-
    tized the xxi die.

B. Mr. Richard Travis the xiij die.

1577–8. Februarie.

C. Elizabeth, doghter of Mr. Walter Rygmaden, was
    baptized the xj die.

March.

B. Sr Henri Hee the xvij die.

April. 1578.

C. Ann, doghter of Mr. Robert Plesington.

September.

B. Edward Morley, Gen.

1578.
Nov.

B. Ux. Mr. Robert Plesington the ij die.

M. Thomas Whittingham, and Jenett the lait wyffe of
    Wylliam silcoke the viij die.

1579. Aprille.

C. John, the son of Mr. Albanie Butler the vi die.

C. John, the son of Mr. Rychard Braiddill the xviii die.

1580. May.

B. Issabell uxr William Kyrkbie de Rawkley the xxv
    die.

July.

C. Marie, the doghter of Mr. Walter Rygmayden the
    xxx die.

August.

B. Elizabeth, the doghter of Mr. Walter Rygmayden the iv die.

November.

M. Mr. John Braiddill and Elizabeth Brockhall the xxviij die.

December.

C. Rychard, the son of Mr. Rychard Braddill.

1580–81. Februarie.

C. Katherine, doghter of Mr. Albanie Butler, the ij die.

1581. July.

C. Robert, the son of Mr. Rychard Shearbourne, the xiij die.

C. Anne, the doghter of Mr. Thomas Tyldesley, the xxix die.

1581–82. March.

C. Philip, son of Mr. Albanie Butler.

1583. September.

M. Thomas Nellson and Jane Rygmanden the xv die.

1586. Aprille.

M. George Answorth,[8] vicar of Garstang, and Sicelie Butler, was married the xiv die.

1586–87. Januarie.

C. Marie, a doghter of George Answorth.

May.

B. Jane ux. Mr. Groncker the xj die.

June.

M. William Johnson and Ann Rygmayden the vj die.

1588. June.

C. Dorothi, doghter of Mr. Rychard Braiddill, the xxix die.

B. John, son of George Answorth, the j die.

1589. December.

C. Margaret, doghter of George Answorth.

---

[8] In the Register this vicar's name is always spelt thus.

1590. September.

C.   John, the son of John Butler of Kirkland, Esq., the iv die.
C.   Robert, the son of Mr. Corles, the x die.

1590–91. March.

B.   John Butler de Kirkland, Esq., the xvi die.

1592. August.

C.   Alice, doghter of George Answorth.

November.

C.   Robert, son of Mr. Thomas Sherburne of Catterall, Esq., the xxix die.

1593. August.

M.   Thomas Butler and Elizabeth Parkinson the xvi die.

1594. June.

C.   Thomas, son of Mr. Thomas Shearburne of Catterall, the xviij die.

1597. December.

C.   Dowthie [Dorothy], doghter of George Answorth, the xxiij die.

1599. October.

B.   Ux^r Thomas Nellson the xxviij die.

January 1599–1600.

B.   Mr James Butler of Kyrkland the xxj die.

July.

B.   Sr John Gibson the iii die.

October.

B.   Blacke John, of the Lodge, the xxvij die.

1611. June.

C.   Robert, the son of Mr. Robert Leeminge of Pekering lyth in Yorkshire (Pickering Lythe), the 11th day.

1612. July.

M.   James Walls of Preston, gentleman, and Mrs. Isabell Travers the 19th day.

1613–14. February.

M.   Mackson Nelsin and Mrs. Ellen Travers the 7th day.

July.

B.   Albanie Butler of Kirkland was buried at Ormskirk Church the 9[9] day.

October.

B.   Albanie Butler de Claughton, gentleman. the 21st day.

1615. November.

C.   Edward, the son of Edward Tildesley of the Lodge Esq., the 14th day.

1616. August.

B.   Robert Plesington of Dimples, gent[n], was buried the 6th day.

1617. May.

B.   M[ris] Catherine Houghton.

December.

B.   Bridget, daughter of Richard Whittingham de Claughton, the 10th day.

1617-18. February.

B.   William Butler, the parish clarke, ult°.

1618. April.

M.   Cuthbert Hesketh and Ann Simpson de Goosnargh the 7th day.[10]

June.

M.   George Mitton, Vicar of Garstange, and Elizabeth Simpson Vidua the 17th day.

July.

M.   X'per Parkinson and Mrs. Ambrose de Plumpton 19th day.

1619-20. February.

B.   Mrs. Travice de Naytby the 6th day.

1620-21. January.

B.   Mr. Mitton, Vicar de Garstange, the 18th day.

---

[9] The Ormskirk Register shows that he was buried in "Mr. Scarbrick's Chancell."
[10] *Dugdale's Visitation* of 1664-5 makes *Gabriel* Hesketh to marry Ann Simpson of Barker-in-Goosnargh. The Goosnargh Register confirms this. "Buried was Ann wife of Gabriel Hesketh in *temp'* March 1649."

1622–3. March.

C. Alicia filia M^{rii} Nicholaii Bray 25th die.

1626. May.

B. Mr. ffifte de Wedaker the 9th day.

December.

C. Augustine, daughter of Nic. Bray prebit^{9}, the 9th day.

1629. October.

C. John, the son of Mr. John Dugdale, Schoolmaster of Garstange, the 29th day.

1630. April.

C. Thomas, the son of Mr. Nich. Bray, Vicar of St. Michael's, the 4th day.

1634. September.

B. Mrs. Anne Butler de Kirkland, Lady of ye towne, the 29 day.

1634–5. January.

C. Rachell, daughter of Isaac Ambrose, the 25th day.

July.

B. Thurstan Tildesley de Stanzaker the 22 day.

1634–5. March.

Jane. ux. Augustine Wyldboore, Viccar mariebatur 2° die et sepultur fuit die 13.

1637–8. Febry.

C. Augustine, the son of Isaac Ambrose, the 11th day.

1638. October.

C. Thomas, the son of Jo. Winckley, Curat (see p. 102).

1639–40. March.

C. William, the son of Jo. Winckley, Curat, the 13th day.

September.

C. Augustine, the son of Jo. Woods, Ludi Magistri de Kirkland, the 24 day.

1645. September.

B. Mr. Knevett, Capt., the 29 day.

1649. June 16.

B. X'per Banistre, Esq., of Preston, the 10th day.

1650. May.

B.   ffrancis, son of Collo[ll] Nic. Shuttleworth, the 11th day.[11]

November the two and twentieth 1653.

Whereas it was appoynted by the Justices of Peace, and Quorum of a privie Sessions, houlden at Woodplumpton, the one and twentieth day of October last past, that Mr. William Parkinson and Mr. William Gervis should vēw and approve of the Ellection of a Register for the Parish of Garstange, made by the Inhabitants thereof, or the greater part of them then present, chargable to the releefe of the poore. And as much as it appears unto mee by certificate from Mr. William Gervis, that Thomas Whitehead of Garstange, in the County of Lancaster, yeoman, had the major part or number for his Ellection of Registershipp, and, notwithstanding, offered several tymes afterwards to accepte of just exceptions from Mr. William Parkinson, w[ch] was neglected tyme after tyme and at last refused.

I doe, therefore, accordinge to the Act of the foure and twentieth of August last past, approve and allow of the sayd Thomas Whitehead to bee Register in and for the sayd Parish, and hath, according to the tenno[9] of the said act, administered the oath of Register unto him. In testimony whereof I have hereunto subscribed my hand the day and year first above writen.[12]

EDWARD ROBINSON.

"Nicholas Poulton and Margaret Sprott, both of Claughton, wth the Parish of Garstang, have caused to *beene* published their intention of marriage three Lords days in the Parish Church of Garstang afforesaid, at the closeinge of the severall morneings Exercise, according to the late act. That is to say, upon the ffirst, eight, and sixteenth dayes of January instant.

THO. WHITEHEAD, Register.

---

[11] Nicholas Shuttleworth was a younger brother of Colonel Richard Shuttleworth of Gawthorp; both of them fought on the Parliamentary side.

[12] An Order of Parliament directed that "Registrars" should be chosen in every parish.

"The above named Nicholas Poulton and Margaret Sprott came and presented themselves before mee desireing to be married, producing a certificate under the Register's hand, of the execution and due performance of the publicaĉon of their intention of marriage, according to the act in y^t case made and pvided. Whereupon the said pties were solemly maried the one and twentieth day of January, in the year 1653 above mentioned, by

EDWARD ROBINSON."[13]

In the same year.   William ffrance of Claughton and Mary Ryley of Myerscow published their intention, "but noe certificate hath hitherto been desired by the sayd parties of this Register."

July 1654.   "John King of Bashawe-eaves within the County of York and Jane Bee of Barniker in the Parish of Garstang," have given the required notice, and "were married 4 Sep."

December 1655.   "Mr. Thomas Butler of Kirkland wth the Parish of Garstange and Mrs. Elizabeth ffleetewood of Rossall w^{tin} the Parish of Pulton have caused to beene published their intention of Mariage three Market dayes in the Market towne of Garstange at the usuall place of publicaĉon betweene or aboute the 'houers limitted to an Act of Parliam^t in that case made and pvided, that is to saye upon the sixth 13th and 20 dayes of December instant, by

THO. WHITEHEAD, Register.

They were married the 1st January 1655–6.

March 1655.   "Mr. Edward Lawrence, Minister of Garstange Parish, and now resident therein, and Mrs. Anne Marsden of Tockholme w^{thin} the Parish of Blackburne, have caused to beene published their intention of Mariage three market days in the Market towne of Garstang."

[13] A considerable number of marriages, entered in the exact phraseology, follow this.

T

BIRTHS.

1653. ffebruary.   Christopher, sonne of Robert Walker of Byreworth, was borne the eleventh day.

Elizabeth, daughter of Richard Sharples of fooler-hill[14]
in Cabus, was boorne the eleventh day alsoe.

BURIALS.

1654.

April.   John, son of Mr. John Brockholes of Claughton, gentleman, was buried the one and twentieth day.

1654.

June.   Elizabeth, daughter of Mr. John Brockholes of Claughton,
gentleman, was buried the ninth day.

September.   Ellen, wife of Mr. John Whittingham of Barniker,
was buried the 23 day.

1655.

April.   Mr. Richard Roe and Ann ffrance, both of Garstang,
were married the 4th day.

August.   Anne, the daughter of Doctr William ffyfe of Weddicar,
was buried the 18th day.

September.   Mistris Isabel ffyfe of Weddicar, Widdow, late wife
of Mr. Thomas ffyfe, was buried the 21 day.

1655.

January.   Lawrence, son of Mr. Robert Plesington of Garstang,
was buried the thirteenth day.

March.   Richard, son of Corronel John Reames, was buried the
eight day.

1656.

June.   Margaret, daughter of Thomas Charnocke of Puddin-pie-
noocke, was buried the two and twentieth day.

November.   Anne, daughter of Robert Walker of Byreworth,
was buried the seven and twentieth day.

October.   Richard, son of Richard Wittingham of Claughton,
gentleman, was boorne the thretreth day.

November.   Richard, son of Captain Richard Whitehead of
Barniker, was boorne the seventh day.

[14] Fowler's Hill.

1656-7.

February.   Richard, son of Captain Richard Whitehead of Bar-
          niker, was buried the twelfth day.

1657.

June.   Mrs. Margaret Bayley, Widdow, dyed in Barniker at her
          son Mr. William Baylton's house, was buried the
          sixth day.

June.   Alexander Dunn, a scotchman in his travel towards his
          own countrie, dyed at John Poulton's of Claughton,
          and was buried the Eleaventh day.

1658.

June.   Hugh Regmaiden of Barniker, a lame man, was buried
          the fourteenth day.

1661.

March.   C.[15] Marmaduke, the son of Richard Whitingham of
          Claughton, the last day.

1663.

June.   B. The Wife of Tho. Brockholes de Claughton, Esq., the
          vij day.

1665.

November.   C. John, a sonne of Robt Ditchfield, Vicar of Gar-
          stang, ye second day.

.1665.

September.   C. A child of Mr. John Sallom de Bilsborough the 2d.

1666.

September.   M. James Norcrosse and Eliz. Pleasington 26th.

1667.

August.   B. Mr. Cuthbert Tyldesley de Stanzaker 13th.

1668.

September.   B. William Whitingham de Claughton 6th.

October.   B. Mr. Pleasington de Dimples 6th.

1668-9.

January.   B. The wife of Tho. Regmaden de Claughton 20th.

1669.

November.   B. A child of Richd ffishwick de Myerscough 15th.

---

[15] A note in *Register* that " C " stands for Christening and " B " for Burial, " M "
for Marriage.

1669–70.

January. *B.* Mr. Robt Pleasington de Byerworth 22nd.

1670.

January. *B.* Mrs. Pleasington de Byerworth 29th.

1671.

April. *B.* Thomas, sonn of Tho. Butler de Kirkland, Esq., 18th.

1674.

March. *B.* Juliana, daughter of Robert Ditchfield, minister, 17.

1675.

November. *C.* Thomas, son of Thomas Whitehead of Claughton, 1st.

1677.

May. *C.* Bridget, daughter of Thos. Butler of Kirkland, Esq.

1677.

July. *B.* Robert Ditchfield, vicar, 10.

1679.

March. *B.* Mrs. Juliana Ditchfield of Kirkland, was buried the 15 day.

A Register of all deceased persons certificates and affidavits within the Parish of Garstang, in the County of Lancaster, according to a late Act off Parliament for buryinge in Woollen, commencing from the first day of August last past anno domini 1678.

    Aug. 3, 1678. Thomas Walmesley of Claughton within this Parish was buried the third day of August 1678, noe affidavit brought to mee within 8 dayes which I certified to the Churchwardens and overseers.

    Aug. 19. Thomas the sonne of John Horsefall of Garstang was buried the 19th day of August 1678, and an affidavit was brought to mee within eight dayes after according to the forme of the Woollen Act.

    Jan. 10, 1678. Grace Phishwick of Myerscough was buried the 10th day of January 1678, an affidavit was brought to me within eight dayes according to the purport off the Woollen Act.

[This Register was kept in this form until 1691.]

Ingram Content Group UK Ltd.
Milton Keynes UK
UKHW020837190423
420422UK00006B/457